Becoming Board Certified by the American Board of Professional Psychology

Edited by
Christine Maguth Nezu ■ *A. J Finch, Jr.* ■
Norma P. Simon

Becoming Board Certified by the American Board of Professional Psychology

UNIVERSITY PRESS

2009

Oxford University Press, Inc., publishes works that further
Oxford University's objective of excellence
in research, scholarship, and education.

Oxford   New York
Auckland   Cape Town   Dar es Salaam   Hong Kong   Karachi
Kuala Lumpur   Madrid   Melbourne   Mexico City   Nairobi
New Delhi   Shanghai   Taipei   Toronto

With offices in
Argentina   Austria   Brazil   Chile   Czech Republic   France   Greece
Guatemala   Hungary   Italy   Japan   Poland   Portugal   Singapore
South Korea   Switzerland   Thailand   Turkey   Ukraine   Vietnam

Copyright © 2009 by Oxford University Press, Inc.

Published by Oxford University Press, Inc.
198 Madison Avenue, New York, New York 10016
www.oup.com
Oxford is a registered trademark of Oxford University Press
Library of Congress Cataloging-in-Publication Data
CIP Data on file
ISBN 978-0-19-537243-4

9 8 7 6 5 4 3 2 1
Printed in the United States of America
on acid-free paper

David,

I am so happy to have met you at Nancy Elman's party. I am happier still to have found a copy of the book.

I hope you find it helpful. I would be pleased to mentor you or to help you find a mentor for the board certification process.

CHARME DAVIDSON

This book is dedicated to the memory and "magic" of Dr. Russell Julian Bent (1929–2008), who served as the past executive officer of the ABPP. His countless contributions as a distinguished administrator, clinician, historian, scholar, author, mentor, and leader in the profession will remain a part of the ABPP legacy. His imprint and contributions are evident throughout the book. We mourn the loss of this dedicated colleague and wonderful friend.

CMN, AJF, & NPS

Contents

Contributors

Russell J. Bent, PhD, ABPP [†]
Dean Emeritus, School of Professional Psychology
Wright State

Linda S. Berberoglu, PhD, ABPP
Private Practice
Minneapolis, Minnesota

Thomas J. Boll, PhD, ABPP
Director, Neuropsychology Institute
Birmingham, Alabama

David R. Cox, PhD, ABPP
Executive Officer
American Board of Professional Psychology

Charme Sturkie Davidson, PhD, ABPP
Private Practice
Minneapolis, Minnesota

Virginia DeRoma, PhD, ABPP
Private Practice
Fairfax, Virginia and Savannah, Georgia

Eric York Drogin, JD, PhD, ABPP
Member, Program in Psychiatry and the Law
Harvard Medical School
Beth Israel Deaconess Medical Center

A. J Finch, Jr., PhD, ABPP
Professor
The Citadel

Robert W. Goldberg, PhD, ABPP
Associate Chief and Director of Training, Psychology Service
Louis Stokes Cleveland DVA Medical Center

[†] deceased

Kathleen J. Hart, PhD, ABPP
Professor
Xavier University

M. Victoria Ingram, PhD, ABPP
Chief, Psychology and Neuropsychological Services
Womack Army Medical Center

Florence W. Kaslow, PhD, ABPP
President, Kaslow Associates, P.A.
Director, Florida Couples and Family Institute

Nadine J. Kaslow, PhD, ABPP
Professor and Chief Psychologist
Emory University

Gregory P. Lee, PhD, ABPP
Medical College of Georgia
Department of Neurology

W. Michael Nelson, III, PhD, ABPP
Professor
Xavier University

Arthur M. Nezu, PhD, ABPP
Professor of Psychology, Medicine, & Public Health
Drexel University
Nezu Psychological Associates

Christine Maguth Nezu, PhD, ABPP
Professor of Psychology and Medicine
Drexel University
Nezu Psychological Associates

Randy K. Otto, PhD, ABPP
Florida Mental Health Institute
Department of Mental Health Law & Policy
University of South Florida

Ralph E. (Ted) Packard, PhD, ABPP
Professor Emeritus of Educational Psychology
University of Utah

Norma P. Simon, EdD, ABPP
Former President, Association of State and
Provincial Psychology Boards
Emeritus Director of Training Programs for the
New Hope Guild Centers
Private Practice (Retired)
Pelham Manor, NY

Joseph E. Talley, PhD, ABPP
Professor of Medical Psychology
Department of Psychiatry and Behavioral Sciences
Duke University Medical Center

Preface

Specialty board certification by the American Board of Professional Psychology (ABPP) is a valuable credential that has long been a gold standard for competency in the profession. The good news for the ABPP organization is that the value of the credential remains a well-known and significant aspiration for competent psychologists who seek to provide reassurance of their competencies to both their colleagues and the public.

One concern however, is that because many competent psychologists may view the process of board certification as daunting, they may hesitate to actually engage in the application and examination process. The result of this collective trepidation is unfortunate for both the professionals and the public who seek their services. Specifically, if many more psychologists successfully completed board certification, they would have their specialty competencies acknowledged, and many more patients would have access to board-certified specialists. In contrast to other professions such as medicine, where the overwhelming percentage of physicians who are licensed to practice medicine are board certified, the percentage of psychologists qualified to become board certified is much lower.

Our goal in editing this book was to demystify the process and encourage all qualified psychologists who offer professional services in any of our 13 specialties to seek board certification. As recent presidents of the ABPP we have answered many questions about certification exams over the years and had to dispel many myths concerning what is involved when one becomes an ABPP psychologist. For example, psychologists are eligible for board certification if they are licensed in a state or jurisdiction and have practice experience in a specialty. They do not have to spend 5, 10, or more years in practice to become board certified. As another example, all ABPP certifications carry equal benefit and weight regardless of specialty area. In other words, an ABPP certification is an ABPP certification! All of our specialty boards adhere to the same policies and standards, and require a face-to-face examination of competence for board certification. While academic and training credentials are important and necessary, board certification is based on the idea that application of one's knowledge to actual practice is additionally required to instill public confidence.

This book was compiled to provide answers and explanations in response to the many questions we have received over the years. It is meant to be a user-friendly guide, with each chapter addressing an important topic and written by an experienced board-certified psychologist. Many of the various specialties are represented by our chapter authors, although the book is designed to be a general guide that can be equally useful to all specialties.

The first chapter offers a historical account of the ABPP and provides the reader with insights regarding the challenges faced by the organization over the past 60 years. While the organization has had both its shining moments and rough roads, the chapter gives the reader an inside look at the development of its significance and the impressive tradition of board certification to professional psychology. The next few chapters focus on questions often faced as one contemplates the ABPP process, such as consideration of when to begin the process or which board certification to seek first. Later on in the book, the chapters are designed to provide helpful advice to the reader on preparation of the practice samples, as well as how best to anticipate the experience of the written (where relevant) and oral examination processes. Finally, the remaining chapters provide excellent guidance on "life after ABPP" and pitfalls to avoid when navigating the journey from initial application to the oral exam.

We are grateful to Oxford University Press for their guidance and assistance in helping this book reach its audience of future board specialists and all those interested in the ABPP process. In particular, Mariclaire Cloutier's experienced and thoughtful suggestions were invaluable as we developed the idea, and Cristina Wojdylo's editorial skills helped provide us with a collective voice.

Finally, it is important to note that each chapter author is solely responsible for all of the information, recommendations, and opinions provided in their chapter. Nothing in any of the chapters represents official opinions of any one of the specialty boards. Although the chapter authors have made their best attempt to accurately describe their understanding of experiences such as the application process, the written and oral examinations, and the associated processes, some information may be inaccurate or change over time. Readers are encouraged to contact the ABPP central office and their relevant specialty board with specific questions about the current application and the written and oral examination processes.

We wish to extend our best wishes to you and encourage you to follow your dreams and pursue your professional goals to the fullest.

Chris Nezu
Al Finch
Norma Simon

Becoming Board Certified by the
American Board of Professional
Psychology

Who We Are: A Brief History of the American Board of Professional Psychology

Russell J. Bent, PhD, ABPP
Specialty in Clinical Psychology

Ralph E. (Ted) Packard, PhD, ABPP
Specialty in Counseling Psychology

Robert W. Goldberg, PhD, ABPP
*Specialties in Clinical and
Forensic Psychology*

Introduction

The American Board of Professional Psychology (ABPP) occupies an important place in the history of professional psychology and in the future directions of the profession. It has played a key role in establishing and defining psychology practice specialties and in developing competency-based examinations that provide individual practitioners opportunities to demonstrate advanced knowledge and skills associated with specialty practice. To document the development of the ABPP, we reviewed selected publications (e.g., Bent, Packard, & Goldberg, 1999; ABPP, 1997a; ABPP, 1992; ABPP, 1998–2007; Mayfield, 1987), acquired personal commentaries by key figures, assembled our collective experiences with ABPP spanning almost 40 years, and perused Board of Trustees (BOT) meeting minutes and notes going back to the late 1940s. The chronological categories that follow summarize important events in the birth and development of the ABPP.

Foundation: 1947–1964

The American Board of Examiners in Professional Psychology (ABEPP) was established on April 23, 1947, as a separately incorporated body replacing a committee of the American Psychological Association (APA) that had studied the formation of a credentialing body for practicing psychologists. The demand for mental health services had increased substantially after World War II. In the absence of national structures or institutions for regulating the practice of psychology, the APA Policy and Planning Board had recognized that "membership in a division of the association . . . cannot serve both as a means of expressing interest and as a certification of proficiency" and that "it was unlikely that membership in the Division of Clinical Psychology could be used as a kind of certification" (APA, 1946, p. 41). It was thus acknowledged that the same organization should not carry out both membership advocacy and professional credentialing functions whose primary purpose was protection of the public. At the time, very few states had authorized the establishment of psychology licensing boards despite the burgeoning demand for psychological services. The creation of the ABEPP was a significant component in the development of professional psychology in the middle of the twentieth century.

Helped by a $2,000 loan from the APA, the new credentialing organization was launched. From the outset, a distinction was made between basic and more advanced levels of competence. The BOT minutes for September 1947 (ABEPP, 1947a), state, "It was the consensus of the Board that responsibility for certification at the 'journeyman' level should fall to the conference of State Psychological Associations. At this time, the Board wishes to reserve its own efforts for the top level certification process" (p. 2). The original board members were Carlyle Jacobsen (president), George A. Kelly (vice president), John G. Darley (secretary–treasurer), John G. Jenkins, Marion A. Bills, David Wechsler, Carroll L. Shartle, Frederick Lyman Wells, and David Shakow. The Board identified three original "fields of certification," initially labeled Clinical Psychology, Personnel–Industrial (which became Industrial Psychology, then Industrial/Organizational Psychology, and finally Organizational & Business Consulting Psychology), and Personnel–Educational (which became Counseling and Guidance and then Counseling Psychology). The September 1947 minutes (ABEPP, 1947a) also reflect that specialty areas were defined by professional activities, and "the titles appearing on its Diplomas should represent the areas of specialty and not the sources of paychecks" (p. 4). Also, the three identified practice areas were conceptualized as "general" specialties. Candidates were expected to show depth and breadth in their field of specialization.

With many psychologists already working in applied-practice areas, the new board members decided to postpone implementation of a formal examination until 1949 and initially identify and credential candidates who met specific professional experience and training requirements without examination. Criteria articulated in the minutes of December 1947 for this initial period (ABEPP, 1947b) were (a) publications, (b) relevant work history, (c) the candidate's professional relations, (d) personal knowledge by board members of the candidate, (e) quality of endorsers and endorsements, (f) prior education and training in both academic work and professional practice, and (g) breadth of training and experience. About 85% of the candidates granted an ABEPP "diploma" prior to the initiation of formal examinations in 1949 held doctoral degrees. The 1947 minutes indicate that board members viewed attainment of an ABEPP diploma "as a safeguard for the public" (p. 513). During this period the Board granted diplomas to 1,086 candidates from a total of 1,557 applicants (69.7% acceptance rate). Even though men outnumbered women substantially in psychology training programs, 48% of the successful applicants were women. During this initial period *all* board members reviewed *all* applications, a staggering task that required 26 separate meetings.

After this initial wave, new criteria were implemented in 1949 that required applicants to hold a doctoral degree, present at least 5 years of acceptable experience, and pass a formal examination to obtain a specialty diploma. In constructing the exam, the Board attempted to combine reasonable cost with use of accepted assessment procedures. The plan included developing both written and oral components to be administered at an interval of several months (a daunting challenge for new candidates!). Objective test items were solicited from "a wide range of interests in the APA including the three primary Diploma fields" (ABEPP, 1949, p. 3), shaped into a written examination by the University of Chicago Department of Psychology with subsequent board additions and adjustments, and apparently pretested in a Veterans Administration assessment project. The first written examinations were administered in October 1949 to 53 candidates and included objective and essay portions designed to tap general psychological knowledge and knowledge of the professional field, with leeway given for individual emphasis on "specialties within the professional field" (p. 3). The candidates sat for 10 hours over 2 days. The first oral examinations were given a year later in November 1950 with three-person examining teams conducting a four-part process that covered (a) a field observation of diagnosis and evaluation skills, (b) a therapeutic intervention presented as a professional practice sample, (c) interpretation and use of research findings, and (d) knowledge of professional psychology organization and practice issues. In the early years, examinations were given annually on a regional basis, in New York, Chicago, Los Angeles, and occasional additional sites. In 1953 the written examination was revised and more general questions eliminated. By 1955 the written examinations were reduced to one 7-hour day, including both objective and essay portions. By 1964 the Board had decided it was not possible to update objective questions continually in order to maintain item validity. The written exam was dropped and the essay component retained.

From 1949 through the next decade approximately 90 candidates per year earned the diploma by virtue of examination. During this period of time, the pass rate for candidates in general ranged from 67% to 90%. The first *Directory of Diplomates*, published in 1953, listed 2,591 psychologists, many of whom had qualified prior to implementation of the 1949 examinations.

The ABEPP was initially supported by an initial allocation from the APA Council of Representatives, which was repaid from initial application and fee receipts. After the first wave of candidates, expenses often exceeded income, and for the remainder of the decade the trustees often requested and were granted annual supplements from the APA.

By 1953 the terms of the original board members had expired and much of the organizational work had devolved from John G. Darley to Noble H. Kelley, who served as secretary–treasurer. Kelley served two terms on the Board and established an ABEPP Central Office on the Southern Illinois University campus. When his term expired, he was appointed the first ABEPP executive officer, a necessary development, given an increasingly unrealistic burden on individual board members. Consideration of adding emerging specialty areas was considered occasionally during the 1950s, including school psychology, child clinical psychology, and the field of "community mental health," but no formal action was taken.

During these initial "founding" years, certification of specialists through the ABEPP was a top-down process. Early on, the ABEPP Board was perceived as a "blue ribbon" entity that consisted of eminent psychologists with academic ties and high levels of professional distinction. During the earliest years, credential reviews depended heavily on references and, often, personal knowledge of candidates by one or more board members, a possibility in the much smaller community of psychologists that existed at the time. When examinations were established, the elaborate, lengthy, and daunting process reinforced feelings of membership in a very special group. Such factors influenced the culture of the organization so that legitimate pride in professional skills and accomplishment at times conveyed an unfortunate impression of elitism that eventually deterred potential candidates and hindered the Board's attempts to expand and grow the number of board-certified diplomates.

"The Gathering Storm": 1965–1979

Sir Winston Churchill's well-known phrase is an apt description of the middle years of the ABEPP's existence. The minutes of BOT meetings held during this 15-year span reflect typical activities of a small professional organization— committee reports, applicant summaries, reorganization efforts, and relationships with other organizations. A pervasive sense of angst and struggle, however, emerges from the printed record as noted by frequent expressions of concern about relationships with the APA, low numbers of applicants, insufficient funds to meet necessary expenses, and fervent attempts to organize and reorganize in ways that would stabilize the organization and stimulate interest in the diploma. Throughout the period the mission of ABEPP was affirmed and reaffirmed as the "pursuit of excellence" in professional psychology. During the latter half of the 1960s, a number of changes were made in examination content and procedures. In 1964 the 200-item objective exam covering "psychological knowledge basic to the specialty" was dropped on grounds that it showed little discriminative power and was not distinctly different from exams given during doctoral training or for licensure as a psychologist. The essay exam continued to be used for a few more years and was designed to measure skill in evaluation, interpretation, and application of research findings. The format of the oral component of the examination was changed also in 1964 so that a single examining committee (rather than three separate committees) evaluated applicant skills in assessment, constructive intervention, and ethical sensitivity. Examiners focused on a professional practice sample submitted in advance and an in vivo interview of a client that occurred during the examination. By the end of the decade, the essay exam also had been dropped, and the content of the oral exam was expanded to include (a) appraisal, assessment, evaluation, and diagnostic skills; (b) change, modification, treatment, and consultation skills; (c) ethical sensitivity and professional attitudes; and (d) utilization of research and theory in practice. Other notable changes included establishment of a procedure for providing feedback to candidates who failed and tailoring of the examination to candidates' self-defined strengths and specific areas of professional functioning. Several discussions occurred during the mid-1960s about the need for a "thorough" task analysis of the work of psychologists in applied settings as a basis for establishing the content validity of the examination; however, because of limited resources, implementation did not occur.

A name change was formalized in 1968, when "American Board of Examiners in Professional Psychology" was shortened to "American Board of Professional Psychology." Active discussions continued regarding the ongoing issue of defining and recognizing various specialty areas. In 1969, "Industrial Psychology" was retitled "Industrial & Organizational Psychology." After it was deemed premature in 1966 and then pilot tested in 1967, a diploma examination in School Psychology was developed and offered beginning in 1968. During the late 1960s there were discussions by the BOT on at least two occasions concerning the advisability of offering only a general credential in professional psychology rather than continuing to provide diplomas in the now four specialty areas. After 5 years of no further entries in the minutes on this issue, there is the following rather startling entry from the 1972 BOT midwinter meeting: "The Board, after long and careful consideration of trends in professional psychology, voted unanimously to offer, starting in 1973, a general Diploma in Professional Psychology. This will replace our current Diplomas which are issued in one of four specific specialties" (ABPP, 1972, p. 3). In fact, no such sweeping change was implemented in 1973 and, curiously, the BOT minutes during the rest of the 1970s make no mention of a generalist credential. It is interesting to speculate on the possible consequences to the ABPP and to professional psychology if the generalist policy had in fact been promulgated.

Frequent concerns are expressed in the minutes of BOT meetings held throughout the middle years (1960–1983) over low numbers of diploma applicants and related budget pressures. In 1968, for example, a discussion was held about the necessity of "upgrading the ABPP Diploma" by encouraging employers of psychologists to institute salary differentials that would enhance the monetary value of the credential. A decade later, in 1978, BOT members were still brainstorming options to increase the number of applications. Various recruitment strategies were considered during these years, including asking current diploma holders to mentor five potential candidates, sending personal invitations to potential applicants, and streamlining the application process for senior psychologists who were fellows of the APA. In 1971, BOT members identified a number of possible reasons for chronically low numbers of applicants, including a perceived high rate of examination failure, the "elitist" stereotype that had come to be associated with the ABPP, low practical utility of the credential at that time, long distances between home and examination sites, and an overly "intellectual" and not practical examination emphasis.

By the late 1960s, it seemed obvious that decentralization was needed to facilitate recruitment efforts, bring examinations closer to potential candidates, and give board members more time to deal with the policy issues. "Regional Directors of ABPP Examinations" were appointed in 1969, but this proved ineffective and was eventually abandoned. In 1972, six multimember regional boards were organized and charged with recruiting applicants, conducting examinations, and channeling information to members of the psychological community within their various geographic areas. These boards—in the Northeast, Mideast, Southeast, Midwest, Intermountain West, and Far West—functioned for 20 years until the major reorganization that occurred in the early 1990s. Regionalization was successful in lessening the previously centralized examination burden, but the hoped-for increases in numbers of applicants did not follow.

During this period, examinations were the organization's only source of revenue, and low numbers of applicants meant minimal operating budgets. In 1965 the exam fee was $30; by 1972 the fee had been raised to $300. In an analysis conducted that same year, the Board determined that 150 exams were needed annually to have a comfortably balanced budget. Since no more than 80 to 90 exams had been given in any previous year, it was clear to all that the organization was facing financial insolvency. A short time later, all diplomates were encouraged to contribute an annual $25 "sponsorship fee" to the organization. A year later the situation had not improved, and the Board began to question seriously the ABPP's viability. Fundamental organizational changes were implemented. A letter was sent to all diplomates describing the seriousness of the situation and urging increased financial contributions and recruitment efforts that would help promote the importance of the ABPP certificate. At the same meeting, first mention is made in the BOT minutes of the possible establishment of a subsidiary National Registry of Health Service Providers in Psychology that might extend the influence of the ABPP and possibly contribute a new revenue stream.

A streamlined BOT (now down to five members) met in New York City almost monthly through 1974 and into 1975 in an effort to renew and revitalize the organization. The APA's Committee on Health Insurance (COHI) negotiated an agreement with the health insurance industry to recognize and use a national registry of psychologists qualified for reimbursement under health insurance policies. The COHI recommended to the APA's Board of Professional Affairs and Board of Directors that the APA establish such a registry through the ABPP. The APA agreed to the request and authorized COHI representatives and the APA Professional Affairs officer to meet with the ABPP to initiate the establishment of a national registry. Following this meeting, in early 1974 the BOT authorized establishment of a Council for the National Registry (later Register) of Health Service Providers in Psychology along with a $15,000 start-up loan. At the same meeting the BOT reorganized itself as a parent board with three related subsidiary boards including (a) an examining board, (b) the Council for the National Registry of Health Service Providers in Psychology (NR), and (c) the National Academy of Professional

Psychology (NAPP). The latter concept had been introduced the previous year as a vehicle for offering professional continuing education seminars and workshops.

The NR Council was quickly organized and by early summer 1974 held its first meeting. By late autumn approximately 4,700 applications from individual psychologists had been received, and the possibility seemed promising indeed of a highly successful subsidiary organization that would provide badly needed supplemental funds. Unfortunately, initial agreements between the BOT and the NR Council were neither clearly understood by both parties nor well spelled out, and by March 1975 the NR Council had paid back the initial loan and declared itself an autonomous organization. At the same time it had become apparent that many problems were involved in developing continuing education programs, and the NAPP was not likely to become a profitable ABPP subsidiary. In April 1975, the BOT restructured again, disaffiliating itself from the short-lived three subsidiary boards, so that full energy could be focused on its original examination and credentialing mission. Eighteen months of intense work on "organizational renewal" had had a disappointing outcome, and minutes of BOT meetings held from 1976 through 1978 continued the chronic refrain of too few applicants, insufficient operating funds, and the need for a revitalized organizational mission and structure.

Transition: 1980–1989

In 1980 the ABPP umbrella included only four specialties: the original three (Clinical, Counseling, and Industrial/Organizational) from 1947–1948 and School Psychology, added in 1968. External pressures were developing for the ABPP to recognize and work with independently organized specialty boards in areas such as clinical neuropsychology and forensic psychology that reflected the increasing diversification of professional psychology. Such pressures motivated the ABPP to move from an insular organization described by some as "elitist" and "stuffy" to a position of greater involvement with developments and challenges facing professional psychology in general. In addition to the emerging specialty question, there were issues associated with the increased complexity and expense of maintaining regional examining boards, the need to involve the broader diplomate constituency in governance activities, the introduction of new examination concepts and procedures, and continuing severe financial problems.

Initially, the BOT resisted recognizing and accepting new specialties, as they anticipated recognition of new specialties by the APA. However, given the slow pace of such potential recognition, the BOT concluded that action by the APA appeared to be years away and that more immediate steps were required. In the early 1980s, the ABPP's moratorium on new specialty recognition was dropped and a formal recognition procedure developed. The recognition process required a comprehensive definition of the specialty, including descriptions of required education and training; an extant research base supporting the effectiveness of the specialty services; a nationally representative examining board; reasonable differentiation from other specialties; and demonstration over a period of time of the specialty board's ability to develop and administer specialty examinations of a sufficient number in accord with ABPP standards. This process incorporated many of the principles suggested by the APA Subcommittee on Specialization (SOS) (Sales, Bricklin, & Hall, 1984) that the APA had failed to adopt.

With the dam of traditional opposition finally breached, new specialty boards began to be added under the ABPP umbrella. Clinical Neuropsychology was formally recognized and affiliated in 1984, followed shortly thereafter by Forensic Psychology in 1985. In addition, applications were accepted from Family Psychology, Health Psychology, and Psychoanalytic Psychology, with respective processing stretching into the early 1990s.

As the new specialties completed the recognition and affiliation process, the BOT had to accommodate the representation of the new specialties into the organization's governance structure. Since the founding years, the traditional specialty areas of Clinical, Counseling, Industrial/Organizational, and School Psychology had no separate governing authorities to whom representatives on the BOT reported. However, the opposite was true for the newly recognized specialties, with each retaining their own formerly independent boards. Each new specialty had one seat on the overarching BOT, and the new trustees were faced with the challenge of identifying and communicating with both the ABPP umbrella organization and the specialty board they represented. Clinical, Counseling, Industrial/Organizational, and school representatives had no such divided loyalties. Further complicating the organizational picture were the multispecialty regional examining boards that had been set up by the BOT several years earlier. Obviously, development of a new governance structure acceptable to an increasingly diverse organization was a top priority, and a systematic review of the organizational structure of the ABPP was initiated. Organizational issues were identified and the ABPP's mission statement and bylaws were revised. Consideration was given in 1985 to structuring the BOT as an "umbrella organization." At around the same time, the Midwest Regional Board sent a "sunset" resolution to the BOT that all regional boards be disbanded. No action was taken on either initiative, but it seemed clear that the ABPP was preparing for needed changes.

As in prior decades, finances continued to be a challenge. It quickly became evident that the establishment in 1979 of a voluntary "dues" request of $15 from each diplomate was inadequate to maintain the organization. Also, the modest examination fees being charged barely met examination expenses, which consisted primarily of the travel expenses of volunteer examiners. And Central Office administrative support provided by the organization was proving inadequate to meet the demands of a growing organization. Up until 1984 the ABPP executive officer had been a doctoral-level psychologist, often employed by a university or service agency. Several of these officers served on a part-time basis. In 1984 the BOT sought to reduce administrative overhead expenses and expand services by moving the central office from Washington, DC, to Columbia, Missouri, the residence of the president of the organization at the time. A non-psychologist administrator (Nicholas Palo) was employed rather than a psychologist executive officer. Secretarial support was increased and administrative services expanded somewhat; however, the concurrent affiliation of new specialty boards guaranteed increasing needs for additional administrative support.

In 1983 a procedure for paying annual dues was established by the BOT that was more typical of a membership organization than a credentialing body. Recognizing the potential conflict of interest, the concept of annual dues was dropped a few years later and replaced with an annual service fee that all active board-certified psychologists were asked to pay. This annual payment is now called an "attestation fee." Each psychologist who is board certified must attest to having a "clean" license (e.g., no disciplinary actions) in order to continue as an active holder of board certification through the ABPP. The payment of annual service fees provided a modest and predictable income that proved to be critically important for the ABPP's survival.

Concern had been expressed regularly about the lack of interorganizational coordination among various national credentialing bodies. In response, the BOT proposed a joint credentialing office and more clearly defined and closer relationships with the APA and the National Register of Health Service Providers in Psychology. The initiative stimulated a joint ABPP/APA–sponsored conference in 1983 on the definition and evaluation of professional competence in specialties. The conference had little impact on the field in general but did influence the ABPP's approach to specialty examinations, including a commitment to more competency-based exams and clearer definitions of specialty practice.

A number of improvements in specialty examination assessment procedures were implemented during the 1980s. Attention was paid to increasing the reliability of ratings of oral components of examinations, and Douglas Bray (then president) introduced the assessment center approach in 1982. Rather than being assessed by the same examiners throughout an oral exam, candidates met with separate teams of examiners responsible for different aspects of the exam. Use of videotaped practice samples was emphasized, and ratings of different parts of the overall exam were pooled in a more standardized fashion. The Northeast Regional Board and the Clinical Neuropsychology Board pioneered use of the assessment center format that was adopted later by several other boards. The neuropsychology board also developed a standardized written examination of required neuropsychological knowledge that candidates were required to pass prior to demonstrating advanced competency skills in providing services to clients. Other examination improvements emphasized during the 1980s included greater emphasis on defining specialty-specific competencies, increased standardization of the credentials review process, and clearer definitions of doctoral-level education and training experiences required of applicants. At the same time, more comprehensive criteria defining acceptable internship experiences for doctoral students were being defined by other organizations involved in the education and training of doctoral students. Such developments stimulated the BOT to reduce the ABPP's general postdoctoral experience requirements from 5 to 3 years. And the increased complexity and diversity of the new specialties shifted more responsibility for definitions and quality control to the affiliated specialty boards.

Other notable developments included publication of the first newsletter of the organization, *The Diplomate*, in 1980, with two issues regularly distributed each year; publication of updated and expanded editions of the ABPP's *Directory of Diplomates;* election rather than appointment by the BOT of new members of regional boards; and the presentation by regional boards of slates of candidates from which the BOT selected new trustees. In addition, some state licensing boards recognized the ABPP in their rules related to licensure reciprocity for psychologists. And the federal government established (not immediately, though ultimately, government-funded) salary bonuses for diplomate status in the Public Health Service, the Veterans Administration, and the Department of Defense.

Renewal and Continued Expansion: 1990–1999

A major reorganization of ABPP came to fruition in the 1990s that included many facets and rested on several basic changes. The four initial specialties

(Clinical, Counseling, Industrial/Organizational, and School Psychology) were each incorporated in 1992 and established their own affiliated specialty boards comparable to the affiliated boards of the newly recognized specialties. Concurrent with this action, the multispecialty regional boards ceased administering examinations and were disbanded. In addition, diplomates in specific specialty areas (e.g., forensic, counseling, etc.) were encouraged to organize member organizations called specialty academies. The concept was that the specialty certification boards, under the umbrella of the ABPP's BOT, would focus on examining and certifying competent specialty practitioners while the related specialty academies would provide services to members that included recruitment of applicants, continuing education, and public advocacy. Thus, there would be no commingling, nor opportunities for conflicts of interest, of the examination and credentialing function with the provision of membership services.

The new model called for the BOT to function as the unitary governing body of the ABPP, whose purpose included facilitating a partnership among the independently incorporated specialty boards. By 1996 the organizational transition was completed, and the BOT was composed of a representative from each specialty board, three presidential officers, and a public member. Individual trustees were selected from two nominations submitted to the BOT by each specialty board. Under the reorganization plan, the BOT continued its oversight responsibility of the central office, provided a forum for resolving problems between boards, formulated policies and standards for the organization, appointed and supported committees, and acted as a spokesperson to the public and the profession. Also, an Ethics Committee was established by the BOT that functioned as an independent consultant to the board on ethical matters concerning diplomates. Through their respective trustees, the specialty boards became full partners in BOT governance functions while restricting their activities to that of examining bodies. Advocacy and continuing-education activities were no longer specialty board functions. Rather, their focus was on managing a national certification examination based on competencies associated with a particular specialty area in accordance with ABPP policies and standards.

A most innovative change associated with the renewal process was the establishment of specialty academies. After 40 years of ambiguity, there were finally clearly defined membership organizations for specialists certified by the ABPP in the various specialty areas. With the award of the diploma, membership was granted to the recipient in the academy associated with the specialty. Members of specialty academies had designated Fellow status and could then become involved in academy activities such as recruitment of new candidates, continuing education, public relations, and professional and political advocacy. The Forensic Psychology Academy's highly successful professional continuing-education program is a notable example. An important new function of academies was to submit names of board-certified individuals to their respective specialty boards of specialists qualified to serve on the specialty examining board as vacancies occurred. Academies subsequently organized the Council of Presidents of Psychology Specialty Academies (CPPSA), whose primary purposes included improving interacademy communication and networking for executive officers and committee chairs across all specialty academies, maintaining liaison relationships with relevant organizations as well as the BOT, and coordinating professional advocacy activities.

While the ABPP was reorganizing and renewing itself, independent external psychology specialty boards continued to work for recognition and affiliation, and by the end of the decade the ABPP had doubled in size from 6 to 12 affiliated specialty boards. In 1991, Clinical Health Psychology and Family Psychology (whose name was later changed to Couple and Family Psychology) achieved full affiliation with the ABPP. The formerly independent Behavioral Psychology Board was recognized and affiliated in 1992, and a few years later modified its name to Cognitive and Behavioral Psychology. After a lengthy review process, the Psychoanalysis in Psychology Board became allied with the ABPP in 1996 and generated 50 new specialists within the next 12 months. The Rehabilitation Psychology specialty achieved full affiliation in 1997 and, despite smaller numbers nationally, generated substantial numbers of applicants over the next several years. These applicants were associated primarily with behavioral health and rehabilitation work settings. And in 1999, the Group Psychology Board completed the affiliation process and became the 12th psychology specialty practice area recognized by the ABPP.

Within several months of their affiliation, all six new specialty boards were reviewing applicant credentials and conducting specialty examinations. Related to these affiliation activities, early in the decade an ABPP task force worked on refining the organization's affiliation criteria that led to the later publication of the formal *Application Manual for Specialty Board Affiliation* (ABPP, 1997b). In the same year, another ABPP task force produced a comprehensive *Standards Manual for Specialty Boards, Candidacy, and Examinations* (ABPP, 1997c) that documented basic ABPP eligibility, credentials review, and examination standards used by all specialty boards as a foundation for their distinctive additional requirements and examination procedures. The *Standards Manual* was revised as needed in subsequent years.

After years of relative isolation from mainstream professional psychology, the ABPP became actively involved in the 1990s in liaison activities with a number of relevant psychology organizations and groups. The change from retiring diffidence to enthusiastic involvement proved over the long haul to be transformational in a number of ways. Active liaison relationships were initiated with the Association of State and Provincial Psychology Boards (ASPPB) and the National Register (NR), and the ABPP president began participating in the annual meeting of the Psychology Executives Roundtable (PER). Particularly significant in such outreach initiatives was the proposal presented by Manfred Meier, Neuropsychology board trustee, at the May 1991 BOT meeting "that (the) ABPP initiate a multi-organizational conference on specialty recognition, with ABPP contributing a substantial amount of money toward organizing the conference" (ABPP, 2007, p. 10). The APA in particular was invited to the initial meeting that resulted in the formation of the Inter-organizational Council for the Accreditation of Postdoctoral Residency Programs in Professional Psychology (IOC). Other organizations joining the IOC in addition to the APA included the NR, ASPPB, Association of Psychology Postdoctoral and Internship Centers (APPIC), Canadian Psychological Association, Canadian Register, and a representative from each ABPP-affiliated specialty board. Through cooperative efforts, a model plan for the accreditation of postdoctoral residency programs was developed. The IOC established a liaison with the APA Commission on Accreditation (CoA) to inform and encourage the CoA to consider an expansion of the scope of accreditation to include the accreditation of postdoctoral residency programs.

At about the same time, and likely stimulated in part by the work of the IOC, the APA began exploring a concept long neglected—developing a mechanism for scrutinizing and possibly recognizing specialty practice areas in professional psychology. This led in 1995 to establishment of the APA's Commission for Recognition of Specialties and Proficiencies in Professional Psychology (CRSPPP) that soon thereafter began recognizing specialty practice areas that were already part of the ABPP umbrella. The CoA amended its Accreditation Guidelines and Principles to include postdoctoral residencies in its scope of accreditation, and in 1999 postdoctoral residency programs began to be accredited. Although the ABPP was not the direct cause of these fortuitous happenings, its influence was significant and related to the earlier decision to involve itself actively and continually with various psychological organizations with common interests.

Toward the end of the 1990s the IOC evolved into what is now known as the Council of Specialties in Professional Psychology (CoS), which meets semiannually, includes representatives from all health-related ABPP-recognized specialties (the consulting specialty board not being represented), and has served an increasingly important role in coordinating and advocating across the entire professional psychology spectrum. As evidence of this, the CoS is now represented on the newly reorganized APA Commission on Accreditation.

During the latter part of the 1990s, the ABPP also was instrumental in establishing the Council of Credentialing Organizations in Professional Psychology (CCOPP). The group included representation of most North American groups involved in licensing, specialty certification, and credentialing of professional psychologists. After several semiannual meetings, a consensus document was produced and broadly disseminated that spelled out general principles and a potential taxonomy associated with the development of advanced psychological specialties.

By the end of the decade, more than 3,600 specialists were listed as board certified by the ABPP. Despite the retirement of many older diplomates during this period, the number of new specialists was sufficient to maintain fiscal viability and to offer promise of an expanding ABPP in the twenty-first century. During the 1970s and 1980s, the number of new diplomates averaged somewhat less than 100 per year. By the end of the 1990s the annual production of newly certified specialists ranged between 150 and 200. These gains resulted in part from the addition of six new specialty boards during the decade as well as from ABPP initiatives to certify senior psychologists well established in the field and to attract psychologists just completing newly established postdoctoral specialty training. After the earlier chronic struggle and frequent disappointment, the ABPP BOT was entering the twenty-first century with optimism and a sense of excitement.

Twenty-First Century Opportunities: 2000–2008

In June of 2000, Russell Bent, a recent president of the organization, was appointed ABPP executive officer, replacing the non-psychologist administrative position that had been in place for most of the prior two decades. Dr. Bent had been a recent president of the organization and was a seasoned administrator, a significant force in the movement toward professional competency assessment, and continually committed to the improvement and promotion of the ABPP. By the next year, the Central Office had been restructured, lines of communication with the various specialty boards had been clarified, professional accounting services replaced earlier informal procedures, development of an ABPP Web site had finally been initiated, a Central Office *Operations Manual* was being compiled, and initial templates had been established to bring reasonable uniformity to the organization's various publications, including all-important information for candidates and the examination manuals of the specialty boards. Having a well-known and respected professional psychologist as executive officer stimulated liaison activities significantly and further enhanced the ABPP's involvement within the national credentialing and psychological communities.

In 2002 the Central Office was moved to Savannah, Georgia, which facilitated an increase in the executive officer's time and presence in the Central Office. Dr. Bent served for 6 years until his retirement at the end of 2005.

In 2006, Dr. David Cox was hired to serve as the ABPP's seventh executive officer by the BOT. Fostering of relationships with the APA and related professional organizations was one primary goal of his new assignment, and Dr. Cox's energy and commitment have further energized the organization and helped place the ABPP in a strong leadership position in the profession. On January 1, 2008, the position of ABPP executive officer became a full-time professional position for the first time in the organization's history, and in June 2008 an expanding central office was moved to Chapel Hill, North Carolina. A summary of all of the ABPP's executive officers is provided in Table 1.1.

Table 1.1 *Executive Officers of the American Board of Professional Psychology*

Executive Officer	Years
Noble Kelley	1952–1970
Mark Lewin	1970–1977
Margaret Ives	1977–1981
Joseph Sanders	1981–1984
Nicholas Palo*	1984–2000
Russell Bent	2000–2006
David Cox	2006–present

*Title was Administrative Officer.

In 1998, the Industrial/Organizational Specialty Board, one of three original ABPP specialties, was designated inactive by the BOT. However, a year later, a small group of motivated and persuasive consulting psychologists proposed a new structure and asked for a trial period. In 2000 the BOT accepted the redevelopment proposal of the renamed "Organizational & Business Consulting Psychology" (OBCP) specialty board and provided start-up support. By 2003 the resurrected specialty had a functioning examination board and had certified a small but consistent number of candidates. The reconstituted OBCP board was declared "fully affiliated" once again, and a trustee representing the group was seated on the BOT.

In 2002 a comprehensive application for affiliation was submitted for a Clinical Child & Adolescent Psychology Specialty Board. The applicant group progressed rapidly through the affiliation process and officially joined the ABPP in 2003. A substantial number of Child and Adolescent specialty candidates have been certified since that time. The new Child and Adolescent Psychology and reconstituted OBCP boards represented the 12th and 13th affiliated specialty boards under the ABPP umbrella. Table 1.2 presents a summary of the 13 affiliated specialty boards.

As noted previously, relationships between the ABPP and many related credentialing and psychological groups have increased significantly over the past 8 years. A liaison from the American Psychological Association of Graduate Students (APAGS) attended BOT meetings in the early part of the decade, and the ABPP has been represented in APAGS-sponsored symposia for graduate students at the annual APA convention from 2001 to the present time. In addition to the organizational outreach mentioned in the previous section, the ABPP now extends frequent invitations and sends liaisons (frequently the executive officer) to the Association of State and Provincial Psychology Boards (ASPPB); the Veteran's Administration's (VA) annual gathering for VA psychologists; and to APA's Board of Educational Affairs (BEA), Board of Professional Affairs (BPA), Commission for the Recognition of Specialties and Proficiencies in Professional Psychology (CRSPPP), and, most recently, the Committee for the Advancement of Professional Practice (CAPP). The executive officer and current present are active participants in the Council of Credentialing Organizations in Professional Psychology (CCOPP). The level of liaison activities has grown dramatically over the past decade, as has the recognition and respect accorded to the ABPP from its related psychological communities of interest.

Table 1.2 *Affiliated Specialties of the American Board of Professional Psychology*

Specialty	Year of Affiliation
Clinical Psychology	1947
Counseling Psychology*	1947
Organizational & Business Consulting Psychology†	1948
School Psychology	1968
Clinical Neuropsychology	1984
Forensic Psychology	1985
Couple & Family Psychology‡	1991
Clinical Health Psychology**	1991
Cognitive & Behavioral Psychology***	1992
Psychoanalysis in Psychology	1996
Rehabilitation Psychology	1997
Group Psychology	1999
Clinical Child & Adolescent Psychology	2003

*Originally titled Personnel-Educational, then Counseling & Guidance
†Originally titled Personnel-Industrial, then Industrial Psychology
‡Originally titled Family Psychology
**Originally titled Health Psychology
***Originally titled Behavioral Psychology

Several changes in ABPP terminology were formalized at the beginning of the decade. The older term "work sample" for describing candidate submissions was dropped in favor of the more accurate term "professional practice sample." Use of the term "diplomate" also was discontinued because of the constant problem members of the public and other professions had in understanding the meaning of this arcane term. The phrase "board-certified specialist" is now found in all of the organization's internal and public documents and is compatible with language used by similar credentialing bodies associated with many other professions. Related to this is the change in title of the semi-annual newsletter, effective with the 2001 winter issue, from *The Diplomate* to *The ABPP Specialist*. Development of a comprehensive and user-friendly

Web site has been a constant goal since 2000, as substantiated by its frequent mention in BOT annual meeting minutes on innovations and additional needed improvements. As this book goes to press we are hopeful that a new Web site will have been launched.

There have been several other initiatives designed to foster more effective communication within the organization as well as to the general public and to other professional groups and individuals. After decades of being conspicuously absent from professional conventions and conferences, the ABPP initiated a traveling ABPP informational booth, which has become a popular and well-received activity. Since 2000 the ABPP booth has been at APA conventions, where hundreds of informational packets are dispensed each year. The booth has become a congeniality magnet for experienced board-certified specialists to "greet and meet" friends and colleagues.

The "ABPP Governance Day," initiated in 2000 and held in conjunction with annual APA conventions, has become an effective vehicle for bringing together BOT members and leaders of the various specialty boards and academies for an informal morning discussion of ABPP initiatives and activities. In the afternoon of the same day, the annual ABPP convocation is held, which now includes a lively social hour as well. And in 2001 an attractive new ABPP logo, created by a professional graphic designer, was adopted and has become a significant and easily recognizable ABPP "brand."

In recent years, several significant policy decisions have been implemented. After the "arms-length" approach to specialty academies of a decade ago, it became increasingly apparent that the ABPP and its specialty examining boards were in need of various kinds of assistance that would be more properly associated with these membership organizations. Examples included recruitment, advocacy, and specialty-focused continuing education. In a reversal of policy, the BOT established in 2005 a new trustee seat, with a 2-year term that coordinates with the presidential term of the Council of Presidents of Psychology Specialty Academies (CPPSA). A representative of the CPPSA was installed on the BOT immediately.

In 2005 the BOT adopted a revised "competency model" that spelled out specialty-practice competency definitions intended to serve as the foundation for all specialty board examination procedures. The move reflected the increasing emphasis on the development of practitioner competencies across all segments of psychology's education, training, and credentialing communities. Chapter 3 provides a full discussion of the competencies currently assessed as part of board certification. These include specialty-specific competencies of assessment, intervention, consultation, and science-based applications (along with supervision, management, and teaching, if applicable), and the cross-cutting foundational competencies of ethics/legal foundations, individual and cultural diversity, effective interpersonal interactions, and professional identification.

In 2004 the BOT determined that, as an umbrella credentialing organization, the ABPP had a responsibility to review periodically the policies and operating procedures of its affiliated specialty boards. Periodic comprehensive reviews were initiated in 2005, with the plan to review two boards each year in approximately 6-year cycles. To complete the review process, two BOT site visitors are assigned. The specialty board under review prepares requested documents, and the site visitors observe actual examinations and meet with specialty-board members. Their report is then finalized by the BOT, and includes commendations and recommendations for improvement. In subsequent years, the specialty boards report back on their quality-improvement efforts.

Currently, the ABPP is a well-organized, dynamic organization that remains at the forefront of specialty board certification in professional psychology. Several initiatives have expanded the benefits for psychologists seeking board certification, including those focused on continuing education, practice mobility, diversity and multiculturalism, and recruitment of new professionals through an early-entry application program.

Regarding continuing education, the ABPP umbrella organization was approved recently as a continuing-education provider by the APA; 10 hours of professional continuing-education credit is now available to examinees. In addition, some of the individual specialty academies are approved continuing-education providers. A first ABPP-wide conference is currently being planned for 2010.

To address practice mobility, a task group has worked for several years with state licensing boards to encourage recognition of ABPP specialty board certification as an endorsement facilitating licensure reciprocity. More than 30 licensing jurisdictions now recognize the ABPP credential, with the large California licensing board being a recent addition. Additionally, the ABPP maintains a strong liaison partnership with the ASPPB.

The organization's task force on diversity and multiculturalism was organized in 2000 and has been active ever since. Using the APA's broad definition of diversity, the task group studied the issue for a year and in 2001 presented several recommendations to the BOT that were subsequently adopted.

Articles in *The ABPP Specialist* have highlighted relevant issues and reported on progress made. Most notably, an entry in the minutes of the 2005 annual BOT meeting indicated that the specialty boards, as well as the umbrella organization, had revised their application materials and examination handbooks to include appropriate diversity content. They further reported that active recruiting was occurring regularly and that diversity topics had been integrated into examination procedures. Finally, the ABPP provides direct support and often participates in presentations to multicultural summit conferences. The furthering of diversity and multiculturalism remains a priority for the organization.

The Early Entry Option for emerging professionals is a recent exciting initiative aimed at doctoral students, interns, and postdoctoral residents, to provide them with a helpful path toward eventual board certification in a specialty. The program stipulates that such individuals may begin their application to the ABPP at any time by paying a $25 fee, with no additional application payments required until the applicant later engaged in the next phase of examination. Applicants can declare their specialty area whenever they wish, and after meeting eligibility requirements can pursue specialty board certification in the usual manner. As part of the program, the ABPP is asking graduate and postdoctoral programs to consider underwriting the $25 fee and to actively encourage students and residents to apply. The program has been available since 2007 and the response gratifying.

To support the future success of the organization, the ABPP recently undertook a long-term strategic planning process, initiated by President Al Finch in 2006, that was concluded at the December 2007 BOT annual meeting. Critical priorities were identified that will guide future initiatives and the present value statement was developed. The strategic planning process resulted in activities that will strengthen the organization's stability, growth, and communication to the profession and the public.

As a summary of the ABPP 's leadership and the specialty fields recognized, Table 1.1 lists all ABPP executive officers, Table 1.2 shows all of the affiliated specialty boards, and Table 1.3 lists all presidents of the ABPP.

Summary

After an arduous and protracted adolescence, in its 61st year the ABPP is now into young adulthood. Reasonably confident, strongly motivated, connected to a network of like-minded colleagues and associations, and well organized

Table 1.3 *Presidents of the American Board of Professional Psychology*

President	Term
Carlyle Jacobsen	1953–1953
Harold C. Taylor	1953–1954
Fillmore H. Sanford	1954–1957
Kenneth E. Clark	1957–1960
Stanford C. Erickson	1960–1964
Alfred J. Marrow	1964–1967
Bernard F. Riess	1967–1976
Harry Levinson	1980–1981
Douglas Bray	1982–1983
Paul King	1984–1987
Allen Webb	1988–1989
Jacquelin Goldman	1990–1991
David Drum	1992–1993
Walter Pryzwansky	1994–1995
Russell Bent	1996–1997
Steven Mattis	1998–1999
Ted Packard	2000–2001
Thomas Boll	2002–2003
Norma P. Simon	2004–2005
Alfred J Finch	2006–2007
Christine Maguth Nezu	2008–2009

and structured, the ABPP and its affiliated specialty certification boards and academies face an exciting and expanding future. The value statement endorsed recently by the BOT and displayed prominently on the ABPP Web site summarizes the purpose and value of the ABPP enterprise:

> Board certification by the American Board of Professional Psychology provides peer and public recognition of demonstrated competence in an

approved specialty area in professional psychology. In addition, ABPP board certification provides the professional with increased opportunities for career growth, including employability, mobility, and financial compensation. (ABPP, 2008)

The words of former Executive Officer Russell Bent summarize well the philosophy and intentions of the ABPP:

It is not the exceptional specialist who should be board certified, but the specialist who is not board certified who should be the exception.

Why Seek Board Certification?

Christine Maguth Nezu, PhD, ABPP
*Specialties in Clinical and Cognitive
& Behavioral Psychology*

Introduction

This chapter will address this question from the perspective of the newly licensed professional as well as of the seasoned and successful professional psychologist. The sections that follow describe the value of board certification with a focus on the particular interests and concerns of both recently licensed psychologists and established professionals. This chapter presents board certification as a logical sequence of steps toward demonstrated competence, ethical responsibility, and confidence in one's psychology specialty practice.

For those readers who are anticipating licensure or were recently licensed, consideration of board certification usually occurs after a very long and costly journey. After a challenging graduate education, there are additional application processes for internship/residency, then postdoctoral training and supervision, and, finally, certification or licensure in the jurisdiction in which one practices. At the end of this process, it is reasonable to ask, "Why seek board certification?" For those readers who have been practicing for longer periods of time and already enjoy strong reputations in professional psychology, it is understandable that they also may wonder about the value of board certification.

The Value of Board Certification

As described in the first chapter, the American Board of Professional Psychology (ABPP) describes the value of its credential as one that "provides peer and public recognition of demonstrated competence in an approved specialty area in professional psychology" (ABPP, 2008). Moreover, ABPP board certification is increasingly associated with more opportunities for career growth, including employment options, practice mobility between jurisdictions, and financial compensation (ABPP, 2008; Sweet, Nelson, & Moberg, 2006). This statement of value grows more relevant with each passing year, as the field of professional psychology grows more complex and specialized. There are now many specialty areas of expertise required for the wide range of professional services that psychologists provide. When deciding to seek services, the layperson can be easily confused by the array of various mental health professionals and specialties available. The most responsible way for a psychologist to represent him- or herself as a specialist to the public, state and commonwealth licensing boards, third-party payers, legislative jurisdictions, and the profession is to be board certified through an organized peer process.

The ABPP has been awarding this type of certification in psychology specialties for over 60 years. As the national umbrella organization for its 13 specialty boards, the ABPP Board of Trustees has been diligent in developing standards, policies, examination procedures, and ongoing self-study to ensure the quality of its certification process. As a result, the ABPP has distinguished itself as a high-quality, professional certification that inspires public and professional confidence. The actual competencies assessed through ABPP certification examinations are described in greater detail in the next chapter. For now, it is important to underscore the point that while ABPP board-certified psychologists may not be the *only* professionals who are competent to practice in their specialty area, they all are psychologists who have chosen to demonstrate their competencies across important areas of practice through a comprehensive, oral, peer examination process. This peer examination process includes several hours of face-to-face examination as well as examination of a sample of the candidate's practice. Moreover, no one is exempt from the examination process. As such, it is one of the most standardized and rigorous examinations of competencies currently available across recognized psychology specialties—a gold standard for the field.

The ABPP board certification process takes several months to complete and involves specific stages of candidacy. Both novice and seasoned specialists may view board certification as a daunting task, as it involves multiple steps toward successful completion. These include general credentialing in professional psychology, documentation of specialty training requirements, submission of professional practice samples, and demonstration of competency in relevant assessment and treatment areas through a face-to-face, oral, peer-administered examination. Although it may be a challenging process, it is also important to fully understand the value of obtaining the ABPP credential so that this value compensates for the investment of the time and cost of achieving it.

Beyond the value of board certification, what are the additional rewards? The list of benefits that follows is summarized from statements and publications provided by individuals from the various specialty boards and academies on this topic, information from the ABPP Web site (www.ABPP.org), and recent ABPP strategic planning activities that cumulatively provide an ever-growing list of benefits for the board-certified specialist.

Benefits of Board Certification

"Brand Name" Peer Recognition

The ABPP is a unique, single-umbrella organization with multiple specialty boards and continual quality assurance review that is recognized by the profession as certifying specialty practitioners in psychology. As discussed in Chapter 1, during its long history of over 60 years, the number of ABPP-affiliated specialty boards and associated academies has grown from 2 to 13, reflecting emerging specialties and expansion of the profession (Bent, Packard, & Goldberg, 1999; Finch, Simon, & Nezu, 2006; Packard, & Reyes, 2003). The 13 specialties in professional psychology (see Table 1.1 in Chapter 1) closely correspond with those specialties recognized by the Commission for the Recognition of Specialties and Proficiencies in Professional Practice (CRSPPP), the committee that reviews and recommends petitions for recognition of specialties to the American Psychological Association (APA) Board of Directors and to the Council of Specialties in Professional Psychology (CoS). In recent years, the CoS formally recognized the ABPP in a disseminated statement describing the ABPP as the only national organization of specialty boards to certify specialists in professional psychology. The continuing process of quality review occurs through the organization's policies, procedures, and standards. There are no exceptions to this process; for example, there are no "grand parenting" or "honorary" certifications. The *only way* to get board certified is through peer examination in one's relevant specialty.

Public Recognition and Reduced Public Confusion

Public awareness of board certification in specialty practice is well known in medicine. As the number of board-certified psychology specialists increases, with greater jurisdictional recognition of the ABPP in the United States and

Canada, public awareness of such specialties is on the rise. It is important that the lay public have a means by which to identify and be assured of competent practice. For example, a cognitive-behavioral psychologist recently reported that often during interviews with various media and public dissemination outlets she has been asked, "How can the public identify a competent cognitive-behavioral therapist?" Individuals, including those in the media, who are trying to inform the public about effective cognitive-behavioral psychotherapies often express concern that there are so many certifications and therapists referred to as *cognitive-behavioral specialists* from which to choose. How is the public to know who is qualified? One important way for the public to gain greater knowledge and clarity on the subject and to recognize competent practice in any specialty in psychology, as in medicine, is through board certification credentials from a board with a high degree of integrity in its procedures.

Increased Knowledge and Continuing Education Credits

The ABPP organization is approved by the APA to sponsor continuing education (CE) for psychologists. Candidates who obtain board certification receive 10 CE credits for passing the exam. The ABPP maintains responsibility for its program and content. Where relevant, there are additional CE credits that can be earned for passing the written examinations in the specialty boards that require them (see Chapter 6 for more information). In addition to receiving CE credits for successfully completing the exam, several specialty academies offer conferences and CE workshops in specialty topics, such as assessment and treatment practices, at a reduced cost to board-certified specialists.

Increased Practice Mobility

There are over 30 jurisdictions that currently recognize ABPP as a credential that will help psychologists establish licensure in the event that they move to a new jurisdiction. Psychologists who, for personal or professional reasons, must move to new geographical areas want to have confidence in their board certification credential to ease the mobility of licensure to a new practice setting. In addition to the ABPP credential significantly easing the path toward licensure in a new jurisdiction, holding of an ABPP board certification in 1 of its 13 specialties also provides an expedited path and reduced cost for application of a Certificate of Professional Qualifications (CPQ) and the Inter-jurisdictional Practice Certificate (IPC), through the Association of State and Provincial Psychology Boards (ASPPB, 2008). The ASPPB has an important liaison partnership with the ABPP that is aimed at increased mobility for qualified practitioners. As such, ABPP board certification, along with the CPQ available through the ASPPB, creates a clear path for psychologists to easily acquire a subsequent license in the jurisdictions in which they choose to practice (Datillio, 2002).

Specific Opportunities for Employability and Compensation

It is not surprising that increasing numbers of employers and health-care systems are recruiting individuals with board certification. Areas of potentially greater employability and increased compensation have already been reported for several specialties. For example, in a 2006 article in the *Clinical Neuropsychologist*, Sweet, Nelson, and Moberg identified the salary advantages of a "board-certified practice." Additionally, in a recent search relevant to clinical neuropsychology, over 30% of employment ads specified that board certification was expected or desired. Clinical neuropsychology has been a leader in promoting the expectation that all psychologists practicing in this specialty become board certified. Similar situations are developing for other specialties as well. In organizations that employ large numbers of psychologists in multiple specialties, there is increasing recognition of the importance of the ABPP credential. Employers such as hospitals and health service systems (e.g., Mayo Clinic, Cleveland Clinic) and organizations such as the U.S. Public Health Service, the U.S. Department of Defense, and the Department of Veteran Affairs are increasingly recognizing board certification. Board-certified psychologists working for the Department of Veteran Affairs are eligible for a significant pay increase. The ABPP is increasing its presence each year at conferences held across the specialties. As more and more employers ask about board certification, the advantages of hiring individuals who have sought peer examination in the important competencies of their specialty's practice become apparent. The more hospitals and health systems require board certification, the more the public will become aware that board certification is important in choosing a professional psychologist, and the more board-certified psychologists will be needed to meet the growing demand.

Personal Benefits

The ABPP Web site lists many additional tangible rewards available to the board-certified specialist. These include a publication venue in *The Specialist*, reduction in liability insurance, and an invitation to participate in the ABPP convocation ceremonies and social reception at the annual APA conference.

People have related many personal rewards of going through the process of board certification that are reflected throughout this chapter. The personal accounts of "knowing that I am respected by my peers," "increasing my clinical skills," "really having the opportunity to understand the ethical principles outside of a classroom situation," and "knowing that my practice stands out to my colleagues across disciplines who understand board certification" are often the most compelling reasons for becoming board certified.

Incredible Collegial Experiences

The outstanding professionals that comprise the current leadership and zeitgeist in each specialty have a unique opportunity to move the profession forward. With greater numbers and greater synergy in the ABPP board and academy activities, there is real potential for positive impact on the profession. This type of reinforcement extends beyond the "pins and ribbons" often donned at professional meetings or the social exchange that occurs at the popular APA exhibit booth and convocation activities. As board-certified specialists, we have the opportunity and responsibility to build bridges between specialties because promotion, evaluation, and recognition of competency are goals that we, as well as the public, all agree are paramount.

Opportunity for Meaningful Contribution to the Profession

If you want to get to know and work with the most impressive people that each specialty has to offer, then becoming board certified by the ABPP is an important first step toward working within each specialty board's and academy's activities. When an individual passes the ABPP examination, in addition to a congratulatory letter from the ABPP central office, one typically receives a congratulatory letter and an invitation to join the specialty academy. Whereas each specialty board assumes the responsibility for carrying out examinations, the academies provide continuing education, mentorship, candidate recruitment, and advocacy. Thus board-certified specialists may work with either their board or academy to become an examiner, or through their academy may participate in continuing education, mentoring, or marketing efforts. The final chapters of this book focus on giving back to your specialty and promoting lifelong learning.

How the ABPP Can Help the New Professional

For those readers who have recently completed their doctoral training, there are many decisions to contemplate over the next few years as a new professional.

In fact, you may be discerning what type of further postdoctoral experiences you want to pursue, where you will eventually live and practice, what the nature and extent of your practice will be, and, ultimately, whether you will become involved in the training and supervision of other new professionals. By this time you have probably developed some clear preferences regarding the type of populations or problems on which you would like to concentrate your clinical and/or research activities. Additionally, you have probably adapted a worldview on the theories and scientific information bases that inform your practice. As you experience the developmental shift toward your independent identity as a psychologist, this is your ABPP moment!

From a developmental perspective, you have gained all the knowledge and requisite experience for independent practice, and taking the licensing exam will be the next major milestone toward completing this process. However, you have not yet had the opportunity for a performance-based assessment of your specialty competencies through a peer examination. This type of examination is important, because although your past studying and hard work will likely take you through a successful licensing examination, independent practice will require that you apply this knowledge in an individualized way to each person who seeks your guidance and therapeutic intervention. Competence in the *application* of your knowledge to each individual, group, couple, family, or consultation requires competencies that balance a respect for method and flexibility, science and art, thoroughness and pragmatism.

This competence is greatly enhanced by periods of intensive self-study in which emerging professionals have the opportunity to look at what they know how to do, why and under what circumstances they do it, what informs their work, how they think, and how they work, to minimize error in their work. Prior to this period in your training, you have had to answer to faculty, supervisors, and training directors. For the first time, through a self-study process, you are now ready to prepare for the expression of your own identity by demonstrating competence in a specialty area that best matches your goals and interest for becoming a psychologist. The ABPP exam represents the culmination of these efforts through a peer examination of these competencies.

Why ABPP Is Important for the Seasoned Professional

Years ago, professional psychology training occurred within the context of a field that was limited in size and scope. Competent professionals trained during this time have had to keep up with the field, with ever-new information to learn and to teach to supervisees. To many of us who have been in practice for decades, the board-certification process allows us an opportunity to give ourselves a gift—by engaging in an introspective self-study of what informs our work, what contributes to our positive clinical outcomes, what constitutes the scope and activities of our practice, and what we communicate to those who train with us. Often individuals who hold key roles in training programs and internships serve as role models for their students' and supervisees' entire professional careers. The importance of this role as teacher and supervisor underscores the value of keeping current with trends and methodologies within the specialty. Through engagement in the process of self-study and taking the ABPP exam, seasoned professionals can serve as an important role model in the goal of life-long learning and continuing education.

Additionally, senior clinicians have learned important and valuable clinical information and can give so much back through their specialty academy's continuing education and workshops. Many specialists have said that there are no better audience members or workshop participants than board-certified specialists. Finally, individuals with an ethnic, social, sexual-orientation, or physical-challenge history that has been traditionally underrepresented in leadership positions in a specialty can serve as role models for those in training and can be an inspiration to new professionals.

ABPP Is an Important Professional Developmental Milestone

As is evident from the previous sections, the ideal training sequence for preparing a professional psychologist involves a general professional or applied post-baccalaureate training curriculum, rigorous training in both the science and practice of psychology, followed by an intensive internship experience that significantly increases the learning of applications of a wide range of psychology methodologies. A licensing exam provides jurisdictions with a way to assess whether a doctoral-trained psychologist seeking practice in the relevant geographic area has the requisite knowledge for this responsibility.

However, there currently exists no universally recognized way to assess the *application* of this knowledge base, as well as the additional knowledge base and applied skills required to practice within one of the ever-expending specialty areas of practice. For example, as a licensed psychologist, I am permitted to practice many types of psychology within my own jurisdictions. However, I also have an ethical responsibility to practice within the boundaries of my competence. The board certifications I hold provide me with a measurable way to be confident that I have demonstrated to my peers that

I am competent to provide services within these specialty areas. Therefore, ABPP board certification represents a very important credentialing step for the professional psychology specialist. The APA Code of Ethics prescribes that "psychologists provide services, teach, and conduct research with populations and in areas only within the boundaries of their competence" (APA, 2002). There are few ways, other than self-assessment, to determine the gray areas of requisite levels of competence to practice in a specialty area. Preparation for, and successful completion of, the ABPP exam is one very substantive and meaningful way to be confident that one is providing services, teaching, and conducting research and supervision within the boundaries of competence.

The flow of training depicted in Figure 2.1 indicates the milestones required for the confident and competent professional psychologist to work within one of the recognized specialty areas of practice.

Following an undergraduate curriculum and graduate education and training (including clinical practica training), an internship/residency provides an opportunity for future psychologists to translate their knowledge in applied settings. However, at this point, the emerging professional is still under the close supervision and training of the program faculty. To assess a candidate's

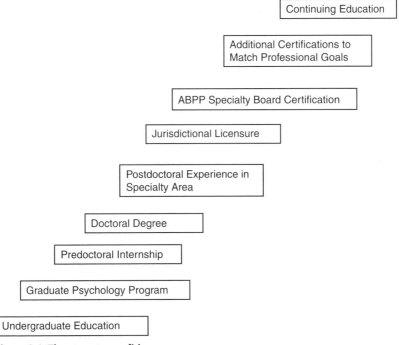

Figure 2.1 The steps to confidence.

level of research and scholarship, doctoral training requires a comprehensive oral defense prior to completing the degree. Yet there are few programs that require an examination of clinical competency with similar rigor. This is understandable, if we consider that students who are completing their doctoral training have not yet satisfactorily prepared for independent practice. Once a doctoral degree is awarded, postgraduate work continues to provide important specialized training, but there is still a structure to which the student adheres. Once licensed, the new professional can now practice independently.

Although peer supervision and continuing education are consistently encouraged in the profession, there are few opportunities for objective, evaluative feedback from peers to complete the process and instill a sense of confidence in one's services. The training model depicted here is one that places the ABPP optimally at this point in time. Successful board certification at this stage in one's career can consolidate interests and goals and serve as a springboard for pursuing additional credentials that match one's goals and direct the lifelong continuing learning process. Such additional experiences might include training in specific technologies or proficiencies relevant to continued and recently advanced work in the specialty.

In this ideal training sequence, the learning process continues throughout one's career with a sense of curiosity and excitement, rather than as a burden. I have heard many of my colleagues say that participating in or providing a board- or academy-sponsored workshop to expand their knowledge in their specialty (or explore other specialties) was one of their most enjoyable professional activities. The ABPP process is a perfect bridge toward this type of professional activity.

Summary

The intent of this chapter was to discuss the reasons for both emerging and seasoned professionals to seek ABPP board certification. I hope the information in this chapter has helped facilitate the application process for those who have yet to experience the value and sense of professional responsibility inherent in the ABPP process. As the field of psychology increases in complexity and specialization, board-certified psychologists will be on the front line of moving each specialty forward and increasing public confidence in professional psychological services.

Board Certification: A Competency-Based Perspective

Nadine J. Kaslow, PhD, ABPP
Specialty in Clinical Psychology

M. Victoria Ingram, PhD, ABPP
Specialty in Clinical Psychology

Introduction

Competence is a core value within the profession of psychology. Ethical practice dictates that psychologists practice within the limits of their competence (American Psychological Association, 2002). Being certified by regulatory and credentialing boards, such as the American Board of Professional Psychology (ABPP), as competent is consistent with ethical practice and conveys to the public the credibility of board-certified psychologists. A focus on competencies assists the public in understanding the roles and responsibilities of psychologists. The competency movement within the ABPP needs to be considered in light of recent advances within professional psychology with regard to a competency-based approach to psychology education and training, practice, and credentialing (Kaslow, 2004; Kaslow et al., 2004; Kaslow, Dunn, & Smith, 2008; Kaslow et al., 2007; Roberts, Borden, Christiansen, & Lopez, 2005; Rubin et al., 2007). This chapter begins by defining the relevant constructs and reviewing the evolution of the shift toward a culture of competence and competency assessment within professional psychology. Attention is then paid to the history of a competency-based approach within board certification in professional psychology, focusing on the current competencies of interest to ABPP's board certification process. It is hoped that this chapter will serve as a useful guide for early career psychologists as well as psychologists considering the senior option, as the competencies that are the focus of ABPP are those consistent with what people learn in training and do in practice.

Defining Competency

A myriad definitions of competence have been proffered, in part because it is more challenging to capture the construct in words than to determine if an individual is in fact competent (Kitchener, 2000). The *Oxford English Dictionary* (2006) offers the following basic definition of *competence*: "state of sufficiency in a given context or environment". Based on this definition, competence, which is a dynamic process, may be construed as being synonymous with ability, adequacy, capability, capacity, efficacy, efficiency, and proficiency. Professional competence has been defined as "the ability to function in the tasks considered essential within a given profession" (Willis & Dubin, 1990, p. 3). A more detailed and increasingly popular definition, offered by colleagues in medicine, states that professional competence includes "the habitual and judicious use of communication, knowledge, technical skills, clinical reasoning, emotions, values, and reflection in daily practice for the benefit of the individual and community being served" (Epstein & Hundert, 2002, p. 226). The crafters of this definition further highlight the fact that competence involves "habits of mind, critical thinking and analysis, professional judgment in assessing situations and ascertaining appropriate responses, and evaluating and modifying decisions via reflective practice" (p. 227). In other words, board-certified psychologists who are competent in their area of specialty evidence capability and demonstrated ability to comprehend and perform certain tasks appropriately and effectively in a fashion that is consistent with the expectations of an individual qualified by education, training, and credentialing in that specialty area and that they do so in a manner that serves the public well.

Competencies, which can be distinguished from competence, refer to knowledge, skills, and attitudes, and their integration. Recently, attention has been paid to defining foundational and functional competencies within professional psychology (Kaslow et al., 2008; Rodolfa et al., 2005). The major foundational domains of competence are considered cross-cutting and include the following: professionalism (Elman, Illfelder-Kaye, & Robiner, 2005: Stern, 2006), reflective practice (Belar et al., 2001; Elman et al., 2005; Hatcher & Lassiter, 2007), scientific knowledge and methods (Bieschke, Fouad, Collins, & Halonen, 2004), relationships, individual and cultural diversity (American Psychological Association, 2003, 2004, 2007; Arredondo et al., 1996; Division 44, 2000), ethical-legal standards and policies (de las Fuentes, Willmuth, & Yarrow, 2005), and interdisciplinary systems. The functional core competencies include assessment (Krishnamurthy et al., 2004), intervention

(Spruill et al., 2004), consultation (Arredondo, Shealy, Neale, & Winfrey, 2004), research and evaluation (Bieschke et al., 2004), supervision (Falender et al., 2004; Falender & Shafranske, 2004, 2007; Kaslow & Bell, 2008), teaching, administration, and advocacy.

Competency refers to the minimal threshold expected for an individual to move to the next level of training or practice or to meet the criterion for board certification in a specialty domain. When ascertaining components and performance levels of competency, delineation of the knowledge, skills, and attitudes that comprise the competence (i.e., benchmarks) is required. *Benchmarks* are defined as the behavioral indicators that are associated with each domain that provide descriptions and examples of expected performance at each developmental stage and that reflect standards of measurement for performance that can be used for comparison and to identify needs for improvement (Kaslow et al., 2006). Within the ABPP board certification process, the scoring criteria used by the various boards reflect the expected benchmarks associated with each overarching competency and its associated essential components to ascertain if the candidate's functioning is consistent with the level of performance expected of an individual board certified in that given specialty. As an example of the expected competencies in a functional domain (i.e., assessment), for competence to be achieved, individuals are expected to choose assessment and evaluation procedures that serve the following purposes:

- Provide data that could answer the referral questions and that are appropriate for all aspects of the client's or patient's diversity status; conduct assessments and evaluations in a competent fashion
- Interpret assessment and evaluation data in a reasonably accurate and complete manner and use these interpretations to guide case conceptualization
- Create recommendations with relevant findings considered
- Communicate, both orally and in writing, findings from assessments and evaluations to the patient and other relevant parties in an understandable and useful fashion
- Demonstrate attention to interpersonal interactions, individual and cultural diversity, ethics and legal foundations, and professional identification as related to assessment.

This level of performance is commensurate with that expected of newly licensed psychologists.

Assessing Competence

There has been a burgeoning of interest in the effective strategies for assessing competence (Bandiera, Sherbino, & Frank, 2006; Kaslow et al., 2007; Roberts et al., 2005) and the principles that should guide such assessments (Kaslow et al., 2007). Assessing competence at the level of board certification helps individuals to consolidate their learning in a particular specialty domain by offering them the opportunity to review and integrate all of their previous relevant learning and experience, provides an impetus for further professional growth, and helps regulate the profession and protect the public (Epstein, 2007). A number of challenges associated with the assessment of competence have been identified, including the lack of consistency within the profession regarding the foundational and functional competencies and their subcomponents, limitations in the validity and fidelity of the assessment approaches, and inconsistencies between evaluators (Lichtenberg et al., 2007). All of these challenges must be addressed as board certification examinations evolve and are made more sophisticated and methodologically sound.

A Historical Perspective of ABPP Competencies

The ABPP has a long history of emphasizing competencies in their assessments and has been on the forefront of competency assessments within professional psychology. In 1983, the ABPP and the American Psychological Association (APA) cosponsored a conference on the definition and evaluation of professional competence in specialties (Bent, Packard, & Goldberg, 1999). As an outgrowth of this joint ABPP–APA venture, during the 1980s, specialty examinations began focusing specifically on specialty-specific competencies (Bent et al., 1999). In addition, this conference laid the groundwork for the ABPP's prioritization of competency-based examinations and competency-centered requirements for the definitions of new specialties (Bent et al., 1999). In 1992, a task force developed operational definitions and procedural clarity with regard to accepting new specialties into the organization. This definition was built in part upon the competency areas deemed to be specific to the specialty (Bent et al., 1999). In 1999, an examination conference was held at which specialty-board presidents and examination chairs formalized changes in the examination process to ensure greater consistency in the examination and evaluation process. This process further served to standardize the examinations across specialties, both for the examiners and the examinees. It also helped to increase the emphasis on competencies within the examination and evaluation process across specialty boards. This ultimately resulted in greater consistency of the examination manuals for the various boards.

When Russell Bent, PhD, ABPP, was ABPP president (1995–1997) and then later its executive officer (2000–2006), he was a major spokesperson for competency-based board certification examinations. His position was a reflection of his prior leadership roles through the National Council of Schools and Programs in Professional Psychology, the educational and training council that made some of the most significant contributions and advances in the competencies movement (Bent, 1986, 1992; Bent & Cannon, 1987; Bourg et al., 1987; Bourg, Bent, McHolland, & Stricker, 1989; Peterson et al., 1992). Dr. Bent underscored the need not only for educational and training programs to focus on competencies but also for this emphasis to be a focal point for credentialing organizations, such as the ABPP.

Following the ABPP's active participation in the 2002 Competencies Conference: Future Directions in Education and Credentialing in Professional Psychology (Kaslow, 2004; Kaslow et al., 2004) and Dr. Bent's contributions at that conference to the creation of the cube model for competency development that integrated foundational and functional competencies and developmental level (Rodolfa et al., 2005), the focus on competency-based assessment within the organization intensified. As a result, in 2005, the ABPP Board of Trustees (BOT) agreed that the same foundational and functional competencies should be assessed by all 13 specialty boards. At that board meeting, the BOT voted unanimously to require all specialty board manuals and examination materials and formats to incorporate and implement the competency model by December 2007.

ABPP's Foundational and Functional Competencies

The foundational competency domains that are the focus of all specialty board examinations are as follows:

1. **Interpersonal interactions**, demonstrated in part through one's ability to relate to colleagues, patients, clients, subordinates, and others in a sensitive, professionally effective and self-aware manner
2. **Individual and cultural diversity**, as evidenced by one's awareness and understanding of one's own and others' individual and cultural diversity (e.g., ethnicity, race, sexual orientation, gender, age) and the impact of such factors on the professional relationship, be that psychotherapeutic, consultative, evaluative, or supervisory

3. **Ethical and legal foundations**, including but not limited to one's understanding and demonstrated compliance with the current ethical principles and practice standards of the APA and the organization in which they might be employed, in addition to the current statutory and regulatory provisions applicable to their specialty area of practice

4. **Professional identification**, demonstrated through affiliation with local, regional, state, national, or international professional organizations, an awareness of relevant existing concerns within the field, and an awareness of one's own need to seek continuing education and training to remain current in an ever-developing profession

The BOT noted that the foundational competencies should be evaluated under each of the specialty-specific functional competency domains.

The functional, specialty-specific competency domains are as follows:

1. **Assessment**, in part demonstrated by one's ability to use a scientific base to thoroughly evaluate a person or organization's collective strengths and weaknesses in an ongoing and dynamic process that may or may not involve formal psychometrics

2. **Intervention**, as demonstrated by one's ability to use proven modalities to effect change in individuals, systems, and/or organizations after a thorough, culturally informed and sensitive assessment has occurred

3. **Consultation**, or one's ability to communicate professional or expert opinion in a manner that engenders decision making and the implementation of those decisions

4. **Science base and application**, as evidenced by one's awareness of theory, research, and practice concerning the specialty area and one's ability to integrate and apply that knowledge in the selection of assessment tools and intervention techniques. In some instances, the ABPP is also provided the opportunity to examine the candidate's own personal contributions to the scientific base of the specialty field

5. **Supervision, teaching, and management**, which is not applicable to all practitioners of professional psychology. However, when it is applicable, what may be examined is one's ability to communicate one's own knowledge in an instructive or didactic manner, one's strengths in navigating the complexities of guiding and mentoring trainees and paraprofessionals, or one's demonstrated abilities in program design, implementation, management, and/or evaluation.

The reader is encouraged to review the manuals for each of the specialty boards on the ABPP Web site, www.abpp.org, for detailed descriptions of the these foundational and functional competency domains. In addition, relevant publications can be consulted (Finch, Simon, & Nezu, 2006).

Assessment of Competence: Guiding Principles

A number of the guiding principles for the assessment of competence highlighted by the Task Force on the Assessment of Competence in Professional Psychology (Kaslow et al., 2007) inform the assessment of competence for board certification in professional psychology by the ABPP. Competencies are conceptualized as generic, wholistic, and interrelated, and developmentally appropriate abilities. The developmental level expected for successful completion of board certification is competence within a specialty domain. The assessments serve as summative evaluations of generic and specialty-specific foundational and functional competencies. The various stages of the evaluation process are designed to reflect fidelity to practice; incorporate reliable, valid, and practical methodologies; and enable a multi-trait, multi-method, and multi-informant process. While the board certification examinations are designed to ascertain whether or not one is competent and meets the minimum threshold expected for an individual to be credentialed as board certified, they also provide an opportunity for candidates to demonstrate their level of capability (i.e., the extent to which competent individuals can adapt skills to new contexts and situations, generate new knowledge, and continue to enhance performance in the face of challenge) (Fraser & Greenhalgh, 2001; Stephenson & Yorke, 1998). Finally, board examiners are trained in appropriate strategies for accurately assessing the competence of the candidates.

Process of Competency-Based Examinations in ABPP

The approach to assessing a candidate's knowledge, skill, attitudes, and his or her integration in the core competencies varies across the 13 specialty boards. However, it typically involves the use of portfolio reviews, ratings of live or recorded performance, as well as oral examinations that include case presentations, discussion of recorded performance, and responses to vignettes. It should be noted that in addition to the components of the assessment process discussed above, two specialty boards, the American Board of Clinical Neuropsychology and American Board of Forensic Psychology, require written examinations that focus primarily on the knowledge aspects of the competency domains being assessed. For the practice sample and oral examination phase, competency evaluation rating forms are completed by assessors who are board certified in the particular specialty.

Many specialty boards use a combination of modalities across a graduated assessment process. For example, the American Board of Forensic Psychology requires a written examination consisting of 200 multiple-choice questions to ensure that persons seeking certification in forensic psychology possess a sufficient breadth of forensic knowledge. Included in the forensics written examination are questions on ethics, law, assessment, and other professional issues. Upon passing the written exam, the forensics candidate then advances to the oral-exam stage, which includes both a practice sample submission and panel interview by three board-certified examiners.

Other specialty boards only include a practice sample and oral examination. For the American Board of Clinical Psychology, both of these phases are competency focused. For example, in the written practice sample, the candidates are asked to detail their activities or accomplishments systematically in each of the foundational and functional competency domains. In addition, for individuals not applying through the Senior Option, the practice sample also requires that they submit recorded performances of themselves engaged in two different functional competency domains. The oral examinations systematically address and assess candidates' functioning in each of the four foundational and four to five functional competency domains.

Given many boards' graduated nature of examining someone on the same foundational and functional competency domains, the question often arises if it is possible for someone to pass a certain competency area in a practice sample phase and then fail later in the oral examination? The answer to this is yes. The critical-analysis and discussion components of an oral examination can reveal that a knowledge base demonstrated in a written exam is superficial and does not translate into the requisite skills or attitudes or the integration of knowledge, skills, and attitudes expected of a successful competency attainment. Or, one's inability to effectively apply one's demonstrated knowledge base to a clinical or professional setting can become apparent in the written or videotaped practice sample. Given this possibility, many boards will apply rigorous passing standards in the competency domains at earlier stages in the examination process, advancing only those who are most likely to be successful in the later oral examination. As noted in the couple and family examiner's manual, "Since the candidate has already passed many arduous requirements just to be seated for the oral examination, it is appropriate for examiners to presume an ability to pass unless the candidate clearly demonstrates otherwise."

Certain competency areas lend themselves well to specific examination modalities. Whereas one's professional identity can often be easily determined through reviewing the candidate's professional statement or vitae, determining a candidate's sophistication in functional domains, such as assessment and intervention, requires demonstration of the skill aspect of the competency. Submitted practice samples, often including the requirement of videotaped professional interactions, help to illustrate this sophistication and serve as a starting point for more in-depth discussions and analysis of abilities during oral examinations. Knowing that candidates have often had the benefit of extensive preparation and consultation on the cases they choose to submit for review, spontaneous provision of standardized practice vignettes during an oral examination is commonly used to assess a candidate's sophistication in identified competency domains. The candidate's ability to "think on their feet" in the face of a novel vignette demonstrates the soundness of their evidenced-based practice in informing their conceptualization, assessment, and intervention plan. Most commonly, the candidate's competence in ethical and legal standards is assessed, in part, through the use of standardized vignettes. Some specialty boards also use vignettes to assess the individual and cultural diversity competency.

As just discussed, certain competency areas are well suited for specific exam modalities. In addition, certain areas of specialty are also well suited to the use of specific tools in the oral examination process. For example, 1 hour of the examination from the American Board of Cognitive and Behavioral Psychology is dedicated to an in vivo professional sample, in which a patient, a role-playing patient, or a student supervisee attends the examination, and the examinee is expected to interview and assess the person, work on a treatment plan, or consult with the person. The person is then excused and the candidate is examined on this interaction.

Candidates should bear in mind that the oral examination process itself is also a viable source of information for use by the examining committee. Certainly an examining committee faced with a candidate who is inappropriately defensive and argumentative in the face of collegial, constructive feedback is within their purview to consider that behavior in assessing the candidate in competency domains involving interpersonal interactions and relationships. The American Board of Clinical Psychology's scoring protocol even allows for this through the requirement that examiners rank the examinee on his or her "demonstrated awareness of self that permits effective functioning in each of the other competency domains."

Although the method in which the competency is assessed may vary somewhat as a function of the specific competency or specialty for which the candidate is examined, emphasis on the importance of assessing each candidate's sophistication in the set of core competencies remains consistent. In other words, although the Organizational and Business Consulting candidate participating in his or her oral examination will not be faced with the in vivo patient experience described for the Cognitive and Behavioral candidate, both will be rigorously evaluated for their ethical decision making, consideration of diversity, knowledge and use of evidence-based theory, professional contributions, and consultative skill in their own specialty professional practice.

Summary

The ABPP has been a leader in professional psychology in creating and implementing a credentialing examination process that is competency based. The ABPP's emphasis on setting competency-based standards and conducting competency-based assessments is not only consistent with the current zeitgeist within professional psychology but also congruent with the focus on competencies in other health professions (Cubic & Gatewood, 2008; Epstein, 2007; Hoge et al., 2005; Leigh et al., 2007).

At the present time, each specialty board examines candidates in four foundational competency domains and five functional competency domains. These domains of competency are considered interrelated, and a candidate who successfully meets the criteria for board certification within a specialty area is obligated to achieve a level of competence expected of a specialist in that area in each of the competencies. As the competencies and their essential components are further refined within the profession, the ABPP and its specialty boards may need to update and expand the competencies addressed during the examination process.

The attainment of these generic and specialty-focused competencies may appear daunting to many individuals contemplating or seeking board certification. However, these competencies are the focus of current educational and training models, as well as standard practice expectations. In addition, individuals are assessed with regard to these competencies continuously throughout the education, training, and licensure sequence. Therefore, while board certification may be another hurdle in the ongoing professional development process, it is certainly one that is quite achievable by well-trained, competent psychologists.

When to Start the Process

David R. Cox, PhD, ABPP
Specialty in Rehabilitation Psychology

Introduction

This chapter addresses one of the most frequently asked questions about the ABPP: "When should I start the process?" The answer to this question is at once simple and complicated. In short, you should apply to the ABPP the moment you decide that board certification through the ABPP is something that you want. Even so, often there is an interval of time between the decision and actually applying.

Many individuals ask the question of when to start, at various points in their professional development. Given that there are certain basic requirements for successfully becoming board certified through the ABPP, many of which cannot be completely documented until at least the post-licensure stage of development, it is understandable that many may wonder when to begin establishing the "file" of documentation necessary for the process. Until August 2007, when the Early Entry Program (EEP) was established, there was no formal mechanism for an individual interested in pursuing ABPP board certification to begin the process until *after* all requirements had been met and officially documented. With the establishment of the EEP, an individual may begin providing documentation as early as during graduate studies. Further details about this option are discussed later in the chapter.

With the initiation of the EEP, there are now appropriate "entry points" to ABPP certification for individuals who are pre-licensure (e.g., students, interns, residents), for early to mid-career psychologists (less than 15 years after attaining their doctoral degree), and for those who have been in the field longer (15 years or more post–licensure). Although each of these entry points has slightly different mechanisms for application and pursuit of board certification, the underlying requirements are largely the same; it is the point in one's career at which one is applying that establishes the essential differences in how to proceed. This chapter discusses the common requirements of all ABPP applicants and issues that may be specific to the applications of those at the various stages of professional development.

The ABPP has two phases of credentials review for determination of eligibility for candidacy. The first is the generic criteria: the set of requirements that is essential to all applicants in order to "get in the door." Following successful meeting of the generic criteria, the application is reviewed for the additional criteria, if any, that are unique to the specialty board. Thus, prior to being able to meet the specialty board criteria, one must already have met the generic criteria. This chapter will not attempt to address the variations present across the specialty boards regarding specialty-specific requirements. Rather, the chapter focuses on the generic criteria—the doorway to specialty certification.

Generic Criteria Common to All Boards

The ABPP has established requirements for education and training that are common to all ABPP specialty boards as well as to all points of entry into the board certification process. These have been in place for many years and with very few exceptions are required of applicants to proceed to candidacy.

Doctoral Degree Requirement

The applicant is required to have completed a doctoral degree from a program in professional psychology that was accredited by the American Psychological Association (APA) or Canadian Psychology Association (CPA), or was a program listed by the Association of State and Provincial Psychology Boards (ASPPB)–National Register (NR) Joint Designation Program. An applicant who is unsure of the status of a specific program may check online. APA-accredited programs are presently listed at: http://www.apa.org/ed/accreditation/doctoral.html. CPA programs are listed at: http://www.cpa.ca/accreditation/cpaaccreditedprograms. ASPPB/NR programs may be found at: http://asppb.org/licensure/license/designation.aspx.

The ABPP recognizes that accreditation of psychology programs became more commonplace and widespread in the late 1970s to early 1980s. Thus, the requirement for graduation from such a program is set for those graduating from programs in 1983 or more recently. Applicants who graduated prior to 1983 and those who believe their education and training meet the essential criteria can make a request for individual review of their education and training for ABPP eligibility. While approval of these cases is on the decline (there are now fewer applicants because of the interaction of length of time from graduation and increased prevalence of accredited programs), there are instances in which it occurs. Thus an applicant who believes that his or her education, training, and experience are worthy of review is not to be entirely discouraged. For example, an individual may graduate from a program that was not accredited at the time of graduation, but became accredited shortly thereafter. The case of an individual graduating in June and the doctoral program becoming accredited in December is one case in point. In *all* cases, official transcript(s) must be submitted for review.

Internship Requirement

The review of generic criteria inherently includes a requirement that the applicant has completed appropriate internship training as well. This is an integral part of the accredited doctoral-degree training program and is essentially encompassed within the process of completion of the doctoral degree. However, it should be noted that not all graduate transcripts notate the completion of the internship on the transcript. Thus, documentation of completion of an appropriate internship is required at the level of review of generic criteria. Whenever possible, the individual considering application to the ABPP is encouraged to obtain documentation of this *beyond* notation on a transcript. All accredited programs provide a certificate of completion; many of the other internship programs will provide a certification of completion and/or at least a letter of completion from the internship site director. This should be provided to the ABPP as part of the application.

As with doctoral education programs, many internship sites are accredited by the APA or CPA. The APA listing of accredited internship and postdoctoral training sites may be located at: http://www.apa.org/ed/accreditation/intern.html, whereas the CPA counterpart is found at: http://www.cpa.ca/accreditation/cpaaccreditedprograms. Other internship sites may be acceptable as well. The Association of Psychology Postdoctoral and Internship Centers (APPIC) lists internships and postdoctoral residency training programs; these training sites are entirely acceptable for application to the ABPP.

Other Credentials

Historically, the ABPP has also recognized the education and training of individuals who hold certain other credentials in professional psychology. A psychologist who is listed in the National Register of Health Service

Providers in Psychology (NRHSPP) and/or the Canadian Register of Health Service Providers in Psychology (CRHSPP) is likely to have met the requirements of the ABPP generic criteria. There are some exceptions to this, although they are not common. The ABPP does require documentation of education, training, and experience of individuals so listed. In rare cases (generally individuals credentialed many years ago) the doctoral training program may be found to not meet the generic criteria and additional evidence of training may be required and/or the application may be denied. The ABPP recognizes holders of the Certificate of Professional Qualifications (CPQ) available through the ASPPB as having met the ABPP generic criteria. CPQ holders are also eligible for a $100 discount on the application fee. As with the other programs, the ABPP reviews documentation and may request additional information. However, the more recent development of the CPQ and the requirements necessary to obtain that certificate has resulted in no such adverse reviews by the ABPP to date.

Licensure

Applicants to the ABPP must be licensed, at the doctoral level, for the independent practice of psychology. Such licensure must be granted by a jurisdiction of the United States, its territories, or Canada. It is important to note that a very few jurisdictions grant a license to practice at the predoctoral level (e.g., a state may grant an individual with a Master's degree licensure at that level). However, such licensure does *not* meet the ABPP generic requirements. The license must be for practice at the *doctoral* level, granted on the basis of appropriate doctoral-level training. The license must be for *independent* practice; licensure that is dependent on supervision or is restricted for some reason is not acceptable for admission to candidacy for ABPP board certification. Individuals who are licensed but have a history of disciplinary action by the governing jurisdiction or of ethical violations (e.g., such as may be determined by the APA) are required to provide details of that history and acceptable resolution prior to review of the application.

Postdoctoral Experience

The requirements for postdoctoral experience vary from specialty board to specialty board. However, the minimum amount of time acceptable is *1 year*; this experience must have been completed through formal postdoctoral training. Alternatively, supervised experience that is not in a formal postdoctoral training program may be considered; however, the minimum requirement would be 2 years of supervised postdoctoral experience. This is an example from one of the ABPP specialty boards. The interested applicant is encouraged to review the specialty-specific requirements as posted on the ABPP Web site: www.abpp.org.

Starting the Application Process

Pre-licensure Applicants (Graduate Students, Interns, Postdoctoral Residents)

The Early Entry Program (EEP) provides a sensible approach to starting the ABPP application process for those who are in training and/or not yet licensed. Such individuals can initiate the ABPP application for a reduced fee (presently a $100 discount), thereby establishing a file with the ABPP. Although the EEP process does not require identification of the specialty board through which one expects to eventually become certified, it does provide for designation. Should an EEP applicant designate a specialty area, the applicant has the opportunity to become acquainted with the specialty-specific criteria early on in his or her training. In so doing, one increases the likelihood that the essentials are met as part of one's early education and training experiences. One could also request that a mentorship be set up with an appropriate board-certified psychologist in the specialty so as to facilitate and guide the process.

An individual considering application through the EEP program should check with the training institution (graduate program, internship site, postdoctoral training center) to see if it is one that has agreed to sponsor (i.e., pay the EEP application fee, presently only $25) the EEP applicant. If so, the EEP applicant has no upfront cost to initiate the application, except for the time and energy it takes to complete the application form. If the institution does not routinely sponsor its trainees, the applicant might inquire that the institution do so. In any event, an individual who is pre-licensure can initiate the application for the EEP fee at any point prior to becoming licensed. Subsequent fees (practice sample and oral examination fees, presently a combined $700 fee) are still applicable at the time of reaching that phase of the board certification process.

Early-Career Psychologists

Individuals who have already become licensed but are still early on in their careers are advised to review the area(s) of specialty in which they practice, the board(s) through which they may wish to become board certified, and the requirements that they need to meet. Often an early-career psychologist has already met all specialty-specific requirements (and the generic requirements), as he or she has pursued a specialty area of practice, without explicitly aiming toward board certification. In this instance, the decision of when to initiate the application is rather straightforward—as soon as possible. Establishing a date of entry into the process serves at least two purposes: 1) it maximizes the likelihood of being fully board certified as early as possible in one's career, and 2) it defines the criteria under which one will be examined. Given the evolving nature of the profession, significant changes do not often occur in psychology. There are changes, however, in expectations regarding competencies, processes of examination, and other areas that affect the process of becoming board certified. Psychologists are examined by means of the criteria existing at the time of application for board certification.

Early-career psychologists who find that they do not meet the criteria for a specific board are in a position early in their careers to pursue the necessary education, training, and/or experience to seek board certification through that specialty board. If one is certain that one will be following through with the requirements, it makes sense to initiate the application even prior to completing the process of additional training. Again, this timing provides the candidate with the opportunity to "lock in" criteria, engage a mentor in the process, and establish a relationship with the specialty board. Often it is through initiation of an application for board certification that one learns of the most efficient or optimal method of meeting the specialty board criteria. On reviewing the application, the specialty board is often in a position to make suggestions about what types of activities (e.g., education, supervised experience or the like) are likely to provide the applicant with whatever is absent in the existing initial application.

Finally, some early-career psychologists (as well as some who are further along in their careers) find that they are interested in pursuing board certification through a specialty area that is different from the one they had previously intended. These individuals may choose to proceed through the board certification process for which they were originally trained (e.g., clinical psychology) and at the same time seek additional education, training, or experience needed for the board in which they intend to become board certified later (e.g., clinical neuropsychology). These individuals are well served to proceed in this fashion. By becoming initially board certified through the ABPP, the psychologist 1) establishes clear competency in one area of psychology, 2) does not need to pay an additional application fee for any other ABPP board certification sought, 3) establishes the fact of having met the generic criteria, and 4) ultimately may become a "double-boarded" psychologist. Many individuals who have undergone ABPP board certification in one area find that the experience of having gone through the process, albeit through a different specialty board, is helpful in proceeding through another one.

Considering all of the above, the early-career psychologist is advised to initiate application with the ABPP as early as possible, when he or she is able to identify the specialty area in which board certification is desirable, even if another certification is expected to be a part of one's future clinical practice.

The Senior Option

Most of the ABPP boards have implemented a minor adjustment to the application process for psychologists who have been in the field for some time. Understanding how the passage of time may 1) affect one's ability to obtain certain forms (e.g., letters from past supervisors, perhaps now deceased) and 2) alter the professional role in which one serves, many of the ABPP boards have attempted to address these issues. The interested reader is referred to the ABPP Web site and specialty board requirements for specifics of any individual board.

What has come to be known as the Senior Option is available through most ABPP boards. This option may eliminate the need for supervisor letters, permit presentation of a somewhat different practice sample, or change the requirement for audiovisual presentation of one's competencies, depending on the specialty board. For instance, a candidate who is more than 15 years beyond licensure may opt to provide a nonclinical practice sample as *part* of the practice sample submission for some boards. For example, presentation of one's line of research, program development as part of administrative responsibilities within a medical center, or involvement in other important areas of psychology may also be considered. It should be noted that this alternative does not *replace* presentation of clinical competency, but complements other clinically based information provided in the process. The reader is referred to specialty board–specific material, as well as to other chapters in this book and other articles that describe the ABPP practice sample. At no time is the examination waved. Every person seeking board certification through the ABPP must take an examination in a specialty area.

Mid-Career Psychologists

Mid-career psychologists generally find themselves developmentally closer to one end of the spectrum or the other, depending on the nature of their education, training, and experience. Some will have undergone a professional development that much more closely parallels a specialty track than have others. Mid-career psychologists are likely able to identify an optimal time at which to apply, on the basis of where they are in relation to those endpoints. For example, a psychologist who "nearly" meets the requirements may elect to proceed with some additional experience or training and thereby more closely parallel the path of an early-career psychologist. Others may find that they will soon qualify for the senior option and will elect to wait for the opportunity to present a somewhat different practice sample than one they might otherwise present. In either event, the psychologist is strongly encouraged to contact the ABPP central office and the identified specialty board, to facilitate the process and make a well-informed decision.

Summary

As discussed throughout this chapter, it is best to start the ABPP application process as early as possible. An exception to this might be an individual who knows that it will take longer to complete the needed education, training, or other requisites than is permitted under the identified specialty-board guidelines. That said, candidates can submit requests for special circumstances and extensions for completion of requirements after they have already applied. When reasonable, these requests generally are granted.

With the relatively recent changes in processing of applications that the ABPP has made, facilitating the process for those who have not yet completed all of the essential requirements, there is really no good reason to wait to start the process. The goal of the ABPP is to *facilitate* the process; this does not translate into making it easier. The process of becoming board certified requires the establishment of one's competency and is, by the very nature of being examined by one's peers, somewhat anxiety producing to most individuals. However, a query to those who have gone through the process will readily reveal that the anxiety "goes with the territory" and is not unique to the ABPP process. Rather, most former applicants indicate that the process is collegial, and many even say that it was enjoyable. Many candidates have stated that the process helped them take the time to assess their practice and think about and conceptualize their work—a process for which there is often little time and yet is very necessary.

Now is the time to start the process. Questions can be directed to the ABPP central office, and staff will put potential applicants in contact with specialty-board representatives as necessary

Finding the Right Board Certification for You

Thomas J. Boll, PhD, ABPP
Specialties in Clinical Psychology,
Clinical Health Psychology,
and Clinical Neuropsychology

Introduction

The question posed in this chapter is which ABPP board certification is right for you. In order to answer this question, a series of preliminary questions come to mind. The first and most obvious one is, "Am I qualified to be board certified?" The second question is, "Does it make sense or do I want to be board certified?" The third is, "How many board certifications should I consider?" Finally, the fourth question to consider is "Which certification is right for me or which one should I do first?"

Am I Qualified to be Board Certified?

If you have read the previous chapter, which provides a well-delineated description of the criteria required for board certification, and are reading this chapter now, you probably have determined that you are "board eligible." As the previous chapter indicates, to be eligible you must have completed your doctoral degree in a professional psychology program and have completed your internship. If you are like most candidates, you have completed a program that has a general emphasis in professional psychology and also emphasizes one or more specialty areas. Many programs have strong tracks in couple and family psychology and child and adolescent psychology. Others underscore various theoretical orientations such as cognitive-behavioral and learning theory, psychodynamic, group systems, or integrated approaches in their training programs. Other professional psychology programs have a strong emphasis in the areas of health psychology or neuropsychology. During internship many psychologists have an opportunity to work intensively in medical centers in the field of health psychology. They may receive substantial exposure to neuropsychological activities, work in rehabilitation centers, or engage in a variety of types of child and adult therapeutic endeavors, many of which are represented by recognized specialties and attendant board certification. It is also very common and, in fact, required in most places that, after completing a doctoral degree and an internship, an individual have postdoctoral training. More and more psychologists complete formalized postdoctoral training in either general clinical psychology or specialty areas such as child, forensic, or health psychology or neuropsychology. If you have a license and are a practicing psychologist it is highly likely that you are indeed eligible to apply for board certification.

Does It Make Sense to Seek Board Certification?

While the reasons for becoming board certified are addressed in Chapter 2, they are pertinent to this chapter as well. The purpose of board certification first and foremost is protection of the public (patients and customers). In this way it is similar to the purpose of licensing. The purpose of licensing is not to give psychologists an opportunity to practice or to collect money from third-party payers. It is to give those who are charged with the protection of citizens of a particular state (the legislators and other forms of government) a mechanism by which to screen, identify, and certify and license appropriately trained and qualified individuals who seek to provide health care in various professional areas. They do this by creating and employing an evaluation mechanism known as licensure or certification. The same is true of board certification. However, as described in Chapter 3, board certification additionally provides consumers of psychology a means by which to identify specialists who are competent in a particular psychology specialty.

Upon entering into practice, a psychologist typically indicates areas in which patients will be welcomed. Those areas likely represent recognized specialties in the field. For patients to know whether the individual from whom they are seeking professional care has the requisite training and has met the standards in his or her field, they need to know if the individual is board certified. With board certification, you, the health-care professional, are informing and reassuring your patients about your background and ability to provide them with the service they seek. There can be no better way to start a doctor–patient relationship than by assuring the patient that he or she is in the right place and in competent hands.

How Many Board Certifications Should I Consider?

Some individuals come at training from the point of view of specialization, whereas others consider generalization to be the most important aspect of the training outcome. Many psychologists think that there is significant value to general training and encourage the development of general skills for as long and as far as it is reasonable and practical to do so. There are general clinical training and general patient care competencies that are pertinent to every specialty.

Many years ago, when several of the specialties were new and just beginning with their examinations, there were individuals who took the exams and failed. In these early years, one of the reasons for failing was that individuals simply did not have enough specialized training in the particular content area. Their training had begun somewhat informally, as there were no postdoctoral fellowships or doctoral programs that provided such specialized training. In the last 20 years, many additional training tracks at the doctoral and internship level have been developed. Postdoctoral training through full- and part-time residencies (fellowships) is now widely available, substantially increasing the number of colleagues with sufficient and appropriate training in the specific knowledge and skills of the various specialties. As a result, the pass rate for the board certification exams across all specialties is significantly more encouraging to applicants.

A second group failed because they knew very well the technical side of the specialty (i.e., neurology, child development, etc.), but their training in the broadest areas of professional psychology (i.e., diagnostic and intervention skill and training in patient care) was insufficient. This was particularly true if the applicant came from a nontraditional or nonprofessional doctoral training program. Even then, and particularly now, it can be problematic for individuals in highly specialized areas who do not have enough general knowledge of the field. Complex issues of inter- and intrapersonal dynamics, environmental complexities, social and habit patterns, and other broad factors that influence one's life, independent of a particular medical or psychopathological condition, have to be recognized, or that circumstance will become an inhibitor to appropriate diagnosis and subsequent treatment. Thus the ability to understand and translate issues of a broad, general nature into the diagnosis and treatment of someone with a condition or disorder in a highly specialized area such as neuropsychology or health psychology is crucial.

Those who are "hyper-specialists" from the beginning may have insufficient general-practice knowledge and skill to integrate specific issues and questions into a coherent whole that takes into account information about the patient outside of the highly focused question. Very often it is the general life problems that manifest in a specialty-like way. For example, with regard to clinical neuropsychology, complaints of memory loss or pain may be associated with medication or alcohol use, decreased health, or increased psychological symptoms such as a phobia or a family conflict. Without attending to the broad underlying factors, several specialists might be like several blind men around an elephant: no one is grasping the larger truth. In a similar vein, understanding adult psychopathology is critical for most child psychologists unless they are seeing children who have no parents. Even when the role of parents, who existed at one point has been changed or diminished, it is likely to be a significant factor. Whether one's therapeutic orientation is cognitive-behavioral, psychoanalytic, or more system based, an understanding of overlapping fields and relationships of medical, pharmacological, psychopathological, social, cultural, environmental and habit-pattern issues is always important. Failure to appreciate these issues is likely to be detrimental to an appropriate professional interaction.

Application for board certification in one of the general areas may represent a good first step in assuring your patients that you are capable of dealing with the broadest range of their difficulties, even if you choose to deal with only one subset of them. It also documents your competence in knowing what to do with them even if you choose to refer them elsewhere. Board certification gives you the impetus to maintain your skills in those areas and continue to develop the strongest possible base upon which to build future specialized certifications and practice.

Conversely, if you are confident that you have received a strong general foundation and incorporated that into a specialty area such as clinical health, cognitive-behavioral psychology, or psychoanalysis, it may make sense to seek board certification in this specialty area first. It may be useful to speak with individuals who are board certified in both the general and more specific specialties to discern which is ultimately the best match for you.

It is common in sophisticated and more sociologically well-developed professions to have at least a subset of the overall group engage exclusively in the practice of a highly specialized area while other members of that same profession practice more globally. Medicine is always a good example because it shares our emphasis on health-care delivery. If one graduates with a generalist degree from medical school (as all graduates do) there are two tracks available. The first is general and often referred to as the transitional year of internship.

The second track involves internships directly tied to the specialty. This is true in internal medicine as well as in surgery, where such specialties as obstetrics and gynecology, neurological surgery, and general surgery begin immediately upon graduation from medical school and require a 5- to 7-year additional training program focused on that area of undertaking. Normally, following graduation from that training program, individuals in neurological surgery, for example, practice neurosurgery but do not practice other areas of general surgery or other specialties within surgery because their training program has simply not led them in that direction. Medical practitioners are thus quicker to refer from one specialty to another when that practitioner recognizes an area of problem or medical concern that is not specific to his or her area of practice. In medicine it is also the case that some specialty areas grow directly out of more generalist training. Plastic surgeons (although there is a mix of training programs here) typically go through a general-surgery program first. Allergists, cardiologists, infectious disease specialists, and endocrinologists typically complete a full internal medicine program and obtain board certification concurrent with specializing in one of those areas, with an additional 1 or 2 years of training (fellowship). In some regions of the United States, and in smaller communities, an individual who is fellowship trained in one of these specialties may well practice the general field of internal medicine some of the time and practice the specialty at other times, simply because of the availability of patients in their area and the need for a broader range of practice activities and to be board certified in each field.

The specialist and generalist practice patterns have also emerged in psychology over the last 25 years. Individuals who go through a neuropsychology program, for example, begin with this emphasis in their doctorate and internship years and during a 2-year fellowship. It is common for such training to lead to practice in neuropsychology to the exclusion of other areas such as psychotherapy. To the extent that neuropsychologists engage in intervention activities, such activity is often tied to the neurobehavioral correlates of a particular patient's injury or illness and not secondary to marital conflicts or long-term neurosis, at least as the primary focus of interest and emphasis. Individuals who have gone through a training program of 5 to 7 years in clinical child, neuropsychology, or health psychology often move directly into board certification in that area. This would be the obvious choice, without much consideration or need for a more generalist type of certification. It would not, of course, preclude the option for taking additional certifications later in particular areas of intervention specialty (Psychoanalysis, Cognitive Behavioral, Group, etc.)

as a way of identifying to patients and colleagues the kind of practice and extra degree of expertise and sophistication that one's practice represents.

Board certification in a general area (e.g., clinical or counseling psychology) is recommended for the general psychologist as well as for the psychologist who finds him- or herself in areas of general practice. It indicates to patients that one is competent in the general area of mental health. This is also true for specialty certification in venue-specific areas such as school psychology and organizational and business consulting. If one completes a program in any of these areas, board certification is an appropriate way of documenting to not only individual clients, but also the organizations and systems with and for which one works that one's training has resulted in the highest level of peer-recognized competency and skill. For a generalist it may be only later that practice demands and opportunities cause one to become somewhat more formally focused.

It is not uncommon for generalist mental health psychologists to become involved in issues related to the legal system. The need to understand the law when consulting with lawyers, the prison system, the judicial system, and police departments may well lead to sufficient training and sophistication (in many cases even including a law degree) that warrants seeking board certification as a forensic psychologist. This certification makes it clear to relevant constituencies that competence goes beyond self-proclamation. It comes with peer-reviewed testimony to the relevance of the individual's personal readiness and of his or her background and training, reputation, and proficiency, as obtained from such an examination process.

This would also be the case if a psychologist focuses his or her practice on, and obtains appropriate training in, areas of various therapeutic modalities (e.g., couples and family, group, psychoanalysis, cognitive-behavioral). It is important to remember that seeking board certification in these focused specialties is not based on whether or not you choose to limit your practice to this specialty. The important issue is to reassure individuals who become patients and to colleagues who may be potential referral sources that a particular area of emphasis, specialty, practice interest, and ongoing activity has been developed to a level at which board certification has been successfully obtained. It is often not clear among general psychologists to whom a patient should be referred for a particular problem or specialty area. As discussed in Chapter 2, board certification makes it clear that the referral is not randomly sent to simply another "good colleague" who might take on a case that the referrer knows is beyond his or her scope of practice. Knowing that someone focuses on cognitive-behavioral or some other area makes the referral much more likely to be informed, intelligent, and efficient.

Specialty certification beyond the general tends to run in two directions. The first is content or venue, and the second is activity. There are a series of content- or venue-based specialties such as clinical child and adolescent, clinical neuropsychology, health psychology, forensic, school, organizational/business consulting, and rehabilitation. There are a number of theoretically based and functionally oriented specialties such as cognitive and behavioral, psychoanalysis, couple and family therapy, and group therapy. These are not internally incompatible. It is appropriate and desirable for someone to be board certified in rehabilitation and neuropsychology, as there is overlap between the two specialties. For instance, when approaching problems with medical patients such as pain management, diet control, or medical compliance from a learning-based approach to treatment, certification in an area such as cognitive and behavioral psychology or clinical health psychology makes eminent sense. This allows for documentation of competence in areas broader than the presenting problem that may well come into play when attempting to deal with the overall circumstance and goes beyond the initial symptoms or complaints with which the patient presents.

One of the certainties of life is that one really doesn't know what one's practice is going to look like or what one's interests and work pattern will be 10 years from now. This fact of life makes a strong argument for certification of the most general type, or for the certification that is most aligned with your doctoral or internship training program. This viewpoint underscores the advantage of preparing for board certification while your training is fresh and in an area where your practice is likely to be launched. As your career progresses and you continue to develop professionally, general certification also represents an excellent background and foundation of competencies upon which to add another specialty designation should that become your focus of practice later.

Which Board Certification Is Right for Me?

It may seem counterintuitive to pursue the most general type of certification. Many people think that the best thing to do is to get as highly specialized as possible as soon as possible. Many will get certification in that highly specialized area and call it a day, with the hope and plan that all subsequent work will be in that area. As evidenced by a career description from one board-certified psychologist, his early career intentions changed significantly over the early years of his 40-year practice, which included a 2-year fellowship in clinical child psychology, followed by 3 additional years' training in neuropsychology. Later, when asked to be director of training of a clinical health psychology program, he became heavily involved in the evaluation of patients being considered for heart transplant, lung transplant, heart–lung transplant, and various emerging forms of bariatric surgery. It would have been difficult to predict at the time he began neuropsychology training that his professional work would require a comprehensive knowledge of the relationship between bodily injury, brain injury, pain, sleep disturbance, depression, and challenging pharmacological management of these related problems.

This example of training goes to the heart of the question for this chapter. An individual seeking board certification needs to choose just one area first, even if there is the realistic probability that he or she will eventually obtain more than one board certification. Given the complexities and interactions of various therapeutic strategy modalities and specialty content areas, how does one pick a place to start?

As with so many things, the best way to make this decision is not by weighing objectively your training and educational background; you have already done that. You know what your degree is, you know where you served your internship, and you know what additional training you have taken. The best way of choosing your specialty area is to know which one you feel most comfortable with. Where would you like to practice? Where do you feel that you will be comfortable practicing and where do you most want to establish yourself as a highly competent, recognized, properly credentialed individual? The answers to these questions will rely in part on the venue in which you wish to practice. In any venue, general training and certification followed by specialty fellowship is common. This is particularly the case in major medical centers. Allergists and endocrinologists complete internal medicine residency first. Plastic surgeons take 5 years of general surgery, then 2 years of plastics and microsurgery. Candidates get board certified in general surgery first, then 2 years post-fellowship in plastic surgery. This process reflects the recognition that a mature profession, socialized toward practice, requires sequential training toward specialty. All knowledge requires a base, and good specialists know more than their specialty.

If you are working in a rehabilitation center, board certification in rehabilitation psychology makes sense, as does health psychology in the setting of a general hospital. In a neurology/neurosurgery program, board certification in clinical neuropsychology would seem to be the right choice. If you are in the department of pediatrics in a school system, in a prison or other part of the legal system, in a counseling system, or in a general clinical psychiatry hospital, it makes sense to consider the board certifications that speak directly to those who are considering you for employment and recognizing you for appropriate levels of competence once employed. As in medicine, many employment centers have a system of privileging. Privileges are granted on the basis of documented training. Board certification in the appropriate area goes a long way toward documenting that training.

A second factor in determining your area of board certification is the degree of uniqueness that may be lent to your situation. If you are in a setting where there are no other board-certified specialists, then board certification will certainly give you a degree of uniqueness and indispensability. Having board certification is a matter of parity, and recognition that your colleagues and employer expect nothing but the best. Additional board certification in an area not yet represented, if within your area of competence, also lends you a unique quality and probably an opportunity to focus your practice. Such certification can help to minimize uncertainty about who gets to do what. If you are in a rehabilitation center with three other board-certified rehabilitation psychologists, board certification in clinical child and adolescent psychology and/or clinical neuropsychology would certainly add favorably to the offerings of the group practice and help reinforce your appropriateness for related referrals.

If the nature of your practice is such that you are likely to be called into court, board certification is even more indispensable. Once again, the appropriateness of the area of board certification to your testimony is an obvious consideration. In most court cases, all of the medical doctors testifying—be it in a custody case, a personal injury case, or a competency case—will be board certified. In addition to content area (e.g., clinical health, neuropsychology, forensic, clinical child and adolescent), some psychologists work so closely with the civil or criminal legal system as to seek specialty recognitions as forensic experts. This designation indicates a psychologist who knows more than just the science of psychology; it indicates someone who knows the law as well. Practice of such specific knowledge and skill (i.e., jury selection, competency evaluation, assistance with legal decisions provided to the court and legal colleagues) can be a full-time occupation.

In the area of public health, psychologists are often involved not just in research but also in policy and clinical undertakings. In school settings, psychologists perform evaluations and provide treatment and consultation in areas such as behavior disorders in and outside the classroom. In general clinical practice, if one is a therapist with appropriate and required training in psychoanalysis, board certification would seem an appropriate way to signal this specialty within the context of practice as a psychologist.

Psychology has emerged to the point where a number of specialty areas have strong training tracks beginning at the doctoral level, extending into a substantial portion of the internship, and merging seamlessly into well-run, organized and recognized residencies (postdoctoral fellowships). Areas such as clinical child and adolescent psychology have had these programs for years, as have clinical neuropsychology, clinical health psychology, and clinical and school and counseling psychology. It is now common for individuals to finish the postdoctoral fellowship and, as part of the actual training process and sequence, apply for and begin the initial aspects of the ABPP examination process.

It is certainly the case that some individuals will proceed in a more specialty-focused direction. They will come out of training programs, take additional training after their internship, and decide that their primary area of interest and training background (cognitive-behavioral, couple and family) are the only ones that require specialty documentation. By having generalist documentation first, one has a broader context against which to evaluate an individual's credentials in the specialty area. It also documents that the individual is capable of taking on the broad range of unanticipated difficulties that any family or group member may reveal immediately or after some time in treatment.

With more venue-specific specialties such as clinical neuropsychology, clinical health psychology, school psychology, and rehabilitation psychology, an individual is more likely to go from an intensive, prolonged and continuous training program into employment in that specialty area. It may be that, given the context in which the practice unfolds, the single specialty designation is entirely sufficient. Psychologists work in a wide variety of medical school settings (multiple departments and multiple internal clinics and institutes). Clinical health psychologists often orient their practice in one direction or another (e.g., diabetes or pain control). The clinical health psychology diploma indicates that they are appropriately trained to take on the challenges of a biopsychosocial nature that exists in medical school practices and for which referrals to psychologists are increasingly commonly made. Further board certification may or may not follow as one's practice evolves and specializes in terms of treatment type, i.e., cognitive behavioral, couple or family, or group.

Summary

The board certification that you choose varies with the type of specialty you begin with. Educational-specific specialties such as clinical child and adolescent psychology or clinical neuropsychology, venue-specific specialties such as school or organizational and business consulting psychology, or one of the interaction-focused specialties often develop as one's practice evolves and matures. With regard to the latter group, its is recommended that a generalist board certification be considered first as a base upon which further designations can be obtained with additional training and practice maturity. For the highly specialized and organized training programs additional certifications may be less valuable, depending on the venue in which the practice occurs. If you are practicing in a specific hospital specialty department or a school system, it is less likely that you will need to add multiple credentials. However, if you are in independent practice or working in a very broad general medical environment, such additional designations may become both practical and necessary. If you are performing medical interventions with groups, as is often the case with alcohol, pain, and weight management, specializing in group psychology is your best bet. If you are a couple or family psychology specialist and your practice involves consultation with court systems around issues of custody and divorce, designation in forensic psychology and training may well be a way of indicating to system clients and individual patients your capacity to take on problems that don't necessarily arise in the normal course of general-practice training.

Board certification benefits consumers (patients and employers), informs our colleagues, and reflects well on us as individuals. Furthermore, it is a way of demonstrating that we practice in a trusted profession with a doctoral-level degree, state regulation through licensing, and national recognition through board certification in our recognized specialties. Board certification is a reflection of our personal growth and the maturity of our profession

How to Prepare for the Written Examinations in Clinical Neuropsychology and Forensic Psychology

Gregory P. Lee, PhD, ABPP
Specialty in Clinical Neuropsychology

Randy K. Otto, PhD, ABPP
Specialty in Forensic Psychology

Introduction

The American Board of Clinical Neuropsychology (ABCN) and American Board of Forensic Psychology (ABFP) are the only American Board of Professional Psychology (ABPP) specialty boards that include a written examination. Both ABCN and ABFP have adopted written examinations to assess candidates' breadth and depth of knowledge in the particular specialty area in an efficient, reliable, and valid manner. Once accepted as a candidate by the ABPP, the written examination is the first step in the examination process for both the ABCN and ABFP. Because the ABCN and ABFP written examinations differ with respect to their development, content, and focus, and because methods for preparation vary considerably, each test is discussed separately in this chapter.

Description of the Written Examinations

ABCN Written Examination

History and Development The ABCN written examination began its development by having practicing ABCN-certified neuropsychologists submit multiple-choice questions covering information that they felt competent clinical neuropsychologists should possess. The ABCN then contracted with the Professional Examination Service (PES) to oversee further construction and validation of its written examination. The PES supervised a thorough process of test development which included item writing workshops, in which ABCN-certified clinical neuropsychologists discussed, reworded, refined, and ultimately approved all questions. This process resulted in a 100-item, multiple-choice test that was adopted as part of the ABCN examination process in 1993. The written examination is regularly revised by the ABCN and PES to ensure that the current version is up to date and relevant.

Overview of Content Areas The 100, four-option (i.e., a, b, c, d), multiple-choice questions comprising the ABCN written examination focus on both adult and pediatric populations, and are based on the core knowledge domains outlined in the Houston Conference guidelines, which include a Generic Psychology Core, Generic Clinical [Psychology] Core, Foundations for the Study of Brain-Behavior Relationships, and Foundations for the Practice of Clinical Neuropsychology (Hannay et al., 1998). Table 6.1 provides a list of topic areas for the Houston Conference knowledge areas.

Passing Criterion The ABCN written examination currently has a passing cutoff score of 70% correct; candidates are informed of their examination scores by the PES. Passing candidates' test scores are not made available to ABCN examiners and do not affect, in any way, later consideration and evaluation of the candidate.

Examination Schedule and Mechanics Candidates must register and pay a $300 examination fee no later than 1 month prior to testing. The ABCN written examination is currently offered in group administrations four times a year at the annual meetings of the International Neuropsychological Society (INS; February), American Academy of Clinical Neuropsychology (AACN; June), American Psychological Association (APA; August), and the National Academy of Neuropsychology (NAN; October or November). The ABCN Web site (www.theabcn.org) lists the dates and locations of upcoming examinations and related information, and all arrangements for taking the examination are made through the ABCN office. A total of 2 hours is provided to take the 100-item test, and there is no penalty for guessing.

Candidates have 7 years to complete the entire ABCN board-certification process after their credentials have been reviewed, and the written examination may be taken up to three times within the 7-year period. Candidates who do not pass on their first or second attempt may take the examination again at any time within the 7-year period after resubmission of the fee in full at the time of retesting. Candidates who fail the written examination three times, or who fail to pass it within the 7-year time period, must reapply for admittance to begin a new 7-year period of candidacy.

Table 6.1 *List of Topic Areas For Board Certification in Clinical Neuropsychology Based Upon Houston Conference Recommendations*

1. Generic Psychology Core
   A. Statistics and methodology
   B. Learning, cognition and perception
   C. Social psychology and personality
   D. Biological basis of behavior
   E. Life span development
   F. History
   G. Cultural and individual differences and diversity

2. Generic Clinical Core
   A. Psychopathology
   B. Psychometric theory
   C. Interview and assessment techniques
   D. Intervention techniques
   E. Professional ethics

3. Foundations for the study of brain-behavior relationships
   A. Functional neuroanatomy
   B. Neurological and related disorders including their etiology, pathology, course and treatment
   C. Non-neurologic conditions affecting CNS functioning
   D. Neuroimaging and other neurodiagnostic techniques
   E. Neurochemistry of behavior (e.g., psychopharmacology)
   F. Neuropsychology of behavior

4. Foundations for the practice of clinical neuropsychology
   A. Specialized neuropsychological assessment techniques
   B. Specialized neuropsychological intervention techniques
   C. Research design and analysis in neuropsychology
   D. Professional issues and ethics in neuropsychology
   E. Practical implications of neuropsychological

ABFP Written Examination

History and Development The ABFP decided to pursue development of a written examination in 1999, and it became part of the examination process in January 2003. The written examination began with a pool of close to 1,000 items that were written and submitted by over 50 ABFP-certified forensic psychologists. Content review of these items resulted in establishment of eight practice content areas:

1. Ethics and professional issues
2. Law and court rules and procedure
3. Testing and assessment
4. Individual rights and liberties
5. Juvenile and family matters
6. Civil matters
7. Criminal competence
8. Criminal responsibility

All items were then classified as falling into one of the eight categories. Next, 15 items were selected (or developed) for each of the eight practice content areas, which resulted in a pool of 120, four-option (i.e., a, b, c, d), multiple-choice items.

In July 2000 draft examinations including these 120 items were distributed to approximately 60 ABFP-certified forensic psychologists who had agreed to participate in the beta testing. Test takers completed the draft examination without study or reference and, although they took the examination anonymously, they did provide important information about themselves and their professional practice and training. A total of 53 scoreable examinations were received and analyzed by September 2000.

With a total possible score of 120, the mean score for these 53 ABPP-certified forensic psychologists was 92 (77%, SD = 11.8), the median was 94, the high score was 113, and the low score was 59.[1] Difficulty values (i.e., percentage of test takers who answered correctly) ranged from 100% to 36%. Correlations between the year that candidates obtained their doctoral degree and the year they became board certified were .44 and .40, respectively (i.e., more recently trained and board-certified psychologists obtained higher examination scores).

The written examination was subsequently amended to include a total of 200 items, with only the 120 validated items being scored for purposes of candidate classification, and the remaining items being pilot tested by test takers. This has ultimately allowed for development of multiple forms of the written examination and continuous item development, testing, and adoption.

Overview of Current Content Areas The current examination has 200, four-answer (i.e., a, b, c, d) questions that are identified as falling into one of seven primary content categories—although it is acknowledged that many questions may fall into more than one category (see Table 6.2).

Passing Criterion Psychologists who were accepted into candidacy before 2008 need to answer 67% of the items correctly to pass the written examination (a little over 1 standard deviation below the mean obtained by the 53 board-certified forensic psychologists; also see above). Psychologists accepted into candidacy after 2007 need to perform in the following manner to pass the written examination:

1. Answer a minimum of 70% of all of the items correctly, and
2. Answer a minimum of 70% of the items for six of the seven categories correctly, and a minimum of 60% of the items in the seventh category correctly.

These criteria ensure breadth of candidate knowledge in forensic psychology, which is the intent of the written test, and will increase the test's ability to identify candidates who are more likely to be successful at later stages in the examination process. Upon completion of the written examination, candidates receive a letter from the ABFP notifying them of their total item score as well as item scores for each scale.

Candidates have three opportunities to obtain a passing score on the written examination. If the candidate does not obtain a passing score on the initial first try, a second attempt may be made no earlier than 6 months and no later than 18 months after the candidate was notified of the results of the first examination. If the candidate does not pass the written examination on the second attempt, a third attempt may be made no earlier than 6 months and no later

---

Table 6.2 ***ABFP written examination content areas***

1. Ethics, Guidelines, and Professional Issues
2. Law, Precedents, Court Rules, Civil and Criminal Procedures, and Judicial Practices
3. Testing and Assessment, Examination Issues, Application of Scientific Knowledge to Legal Procedure
4. Civil Competence, Individual Rights and Liberties, Workplace Discrimination and Employment Rights
5. Juvenile, Parenting, and Family/Domestic/Matrimonial Matters
6. Civil Damages, Personal Injury, Disability, and Workers Compensation
7. Criminal Competence and Criminal Responsibility

---

than 18 months after being notified of the results of the second examination. If the candidate does not obtain a passing score on the written examination on the third attempt, candidacy is terminated, and the psychologist is eligible to reapply for candidacy no earlier than 12 months after the third examination has been failed.

Examination Schedule and Mechanics Candidates must complete the written examination within 12 months of being accepted for candidacy and prepay a test fee to the ABPP. A total of 3.5 hours is provided to take the 200-item test, and there is no penalty for guessing.

To facilitate timely administration of the written examination and reduce candidates' travel costs, a number of ABFP diplomates administer the examination in their professional offices, which are geographically distributed around the United States. The ABFP corresponding secretary is responsible for scheduling and scoring the examination, and providing results to the candidate and ABFP board of directors.

Resources for Written Examination Preparation

ABCN Written Examination

ABCN Candidate Manual All candidates should begin the board examination process by downloading the *ABCN Candidate Manual* from the ABCN Web site (www.theabcn.org) and the American Academy of Clinical Neuropsychology's (AACN) *Study Guide* from the AACN Web site (www.theaacn. org/study/). The *ABCN Candidate Manual* explains the administrative aspects of the process. It outlines the eligibility requirements for candidacy, describes the application process, and provides details about the written examination, practice samples, and the oral examination. The manual also has all the necessary application forms (in the appendices) and contact information for ABPP and ABCN staff available to answer questions about any aspect of the examination process. An additional resource offering practical advice on how to prepare for all portions of the ABPP/ABCN examination is the book by Armstrong and colleagues (2008), *Board Certification in Clinical Neuropsychology: A Guide to Becoming ABPP/ABCN Certified Without Sacrificing Your Sanity.*

AACN Study Guide The *AACN Study Guide* is filled with practical advice to assist candidates as they complete each portion of the examination. The current version is a 76-page document written by well-known ABCN-certified neuropsychologists with chapters devoted to the application process, the written examination, practice samples, and the oral examination (one chapter about the practice sample and fact-finding components and another chapter with details of the ethics/professional commitment portion of the oral exam). There are also chapters devoted to preparing for the ABCN examination and information and advice about repeating the oral examination (see www. theaacn.org/study/).

ABCN Board Examination Continuing Education Workshops Continuing education workshops focused on the ABCN examination process are typically offered several times each year, usually in conjunction with professional meetings (e.g., NAN in October, AACN in June). These workshops help potential candidates learn and ask questions about the examination process, and offer guidance about studying and preparing for each phase of the examination, including the written exam. These workshops were designed to encourage qualified candidates to apply for board certification by demystifying the process and providing strategies for and practical advice about examination preparation.

AACN Mentorship Program The AACN sponsors a mentorship program for candidates who have had their credentials accepted by the ABPP and ABCN. Candidates may request a mentor to help them prepare for each phase of the examination by contacting the director of the AACN mentorship program. Contact information for the director of the mentorship program may be found at the AACN's Web site under the subheading, Study Materials (www. theaacn.org/study/). Mentors are ABPP-ABCN board-certified neuropsychologists who have agreed to donate a limited portion of their time to help candidates prepare for the written examination, select cases for their practice samples, and participate in mock oral examinations. Participation in the AACN mentorship program is voluntary and not required of candidates. The assistance of a mentor, however, may be of considerable assistance. A current description of the AACN mentorship program may be found on the AACN Web site.

The BRAIN Support Group The "Be Ready for ABPP In Neuropsychology" (BRAIN) study group began in 2001 with a small group of friends who wished to help prepare each other for the ABCN board examinations by dividing the workload in developing chapter summaries and topic outlines, organizing formal study schedules, and supporting each other through the process. Over the next several years, BRAIN grew to include hundreds of members so that a leadership structure was formed, a formal e-mail list serve was established, and a Web site was developed to house the study materials and organize various subgroups. The BRAIN study group then entered into a formal relationship with the AACN. The two organizations coordinate educational activities and support one another in other ways as well. There is no formal association between BRAIN and ABPP, ABCN, or any other credentialing organization.

The BRAIN Web site is hosted through the neuropsychology program at Cincinnati Children's Medical Center and may be accessed via: http://www. cincinnatichildrens.org/svc/alpha/n/neurobehavioral/brain. The neuropsychology program at Cincinnati Children's makes no guarantees about the quality or accuracy of the content of the study materials. Staff members monitor the Web site for appropriateness of content and periodically scan the files with updated anti-virus software.

Neuropsychologists need not be members of BRAIN to access and use the study materials housed online. Some of the resources currently available include outlines, notes, study schedules, flashcards, and mock written examinations that are periodically updated by BRAIN members. Those seeking to join BRAIN should contact the membership coordinator (contact information is available on the Web site). Members must be licensed psychologists and have a "sponsor" who is either already a member of BRAIN or who has been board certified through ABPP-ABCN.

Some neuropsychologists join BRAIN before they have submitted an application for review of their credentials by ABPP and ABCN, whereas others are active candidates. There are also members who have successfully completed the ABCN certification process yet stay active in BRAIN to assist others. Although membership in BRAIN is not required to use the study resources on the organization's Web site, there are many advantages to formalizing membership (for which there is no fee) and using the BRAIN e-mail list serve. For example, BRAIN has established a committee to help candidates connect with peers who are at similar stages in the certification process. Once candidates are affiliated with a study group, the activities of the group help them stay focused on the task at hand through regular assignments, weekly phone calls, or e-mail. These study support groups may also provide a sense of encouragement and collegial peer pressure to continue with the study and certification process.

Another benefit of BRAIN membership is the regular contact with other neuropsychologists whose areas of expertise are different from one's own. This is particularly valuable when preparing to take the written examination, which likely surveys for at least some knowledge outside of one's typical area of professional focus. Others in the board certification process can help answer many questions about how the process actually works and how to best to prepare for each component of the examination. Such contact can also encourage candidates to complete the process and reduce the anxiety of the examination process more generally. In addition, there are targeted support groups within BRAIN for candidates in various phases of the examination. There are even support groups designated for those who may be repeating a stage of the examination, which has been a fairly common occurrence.

ABFP Written Examination

ABFP Online Resources The ABFP Web site (www.abfp.com) is the single best resource for psychologists considering applying for board certification and for accepted candidates. A detailed introduction and overview of the ABFP and all stages of the board certification process, ranging from eligibility to the oral examination, can be found at www.abfp.com/certification.asp, and a detailed description of the written examination is located at: www.abfp.com/pdfs/certification/WrittenExamination.pdf. The ABFP Web site provides contact information for ABFP board members who can answer questions that candidates or prospective candidates may have about the certification process, as well as helpful flow charts.

ABFP Suggested Reading List for Written and Oral Examinations The ABFP has developed a regularly updated reading list of books, seminal articles, and legal cases for candidates preparing for the written and oral examinations. The readings are organized around the following topic areas, a number of which are similar to the content areas of the written examination:

- Ethics, Guidelines, Professional Issues, and Duties
- Law, Precedents, Court Rules, Civil and Criminal Procedure
- Testing, Assessment, Judgment and Bias, Examination Issues
- Civil Competencies, Personal Injury and Civil Damages
- Child Custody and Parenting
- Child Abuse and Neglect
- Criminal Competencies, Criminal Responsibility

Identified for almost every topic area are core readings and supplementary readings.

A cursory review of the 10-page, two-column reading list makes it obvious that no one would be expected to read all of the references cited. Rather, it is recommended that candidates use the list to identify references to ameliorate their particular gaps in knowledge.[2]

American Academy of Forensic Psychology Continuing Education Workshops Although the ABFP does not offer any continuing education (CE) workshops, its affiliate, the American Academy of Forensic Psychology (AAFP, www.aafp.ws), has sponsored a successful CE workshop program over the past 20 years (www.aafpworkshops.com). Workshop series are held in up to seven different cities in North America and the Caribbean each year, with as many as 10 different daylong programs offered on topics as varied as child custody and parenting evaluations, expert testimony and report writing, capital sentencing evaluations, jury selection, and violence risk assessment. Daylong workshops devoted to preparing for board certification, which typically have low registration and allow for a considerable amount of interaction with the presenter, are often helpful to psychologists contemplating or in the early part of the board certification process. Also of particular relevance to those involved in the board certification process are intensive and focused 3-day workshops that survey a large number of forensic practice areas.

Preparation Methods for the Written Examination

Preparation for the ABCN Written Examination

Preparation should begin at least several months before the written examination is scheduled and involve an in-depth review of the knowledge base domains listed in Table 6.1. Studying will provide candidates an opportunity to consolidate information already learned in graduate school and during specialty training experiences, and master new information that may have been underemphasized during training. It is important not to overprepare in a single area, especially in an area of particular interest or expertise. Rather, try to focus on areas with which you are less familiar or knowledgeable.

Many candidates tend to overemphasize the neurosciences during their preparation for the written examination. It is important not to neglect the more basic generic psychology and generic clinical psychology topics (see Table 6.1) learned in graduate school, such as psychometrics, reliability and validity, psychopathology, personality, diagnosis, ethics, the history of psychology, and the diagnostic nomenclature in the latest version of the *Diagnostic and Statistical Manual of Mental Disorders* (DSM-IV-TR; American Psychiatric Association, 2000). Many have found simple rote learning useful in preparing for the multiple-choice examination by using flash cards for studying various syndromes, eponyms, clinical signs, cranial nerves, major sensory and motor tracts, and intrinsic pathways within the brain. Such flash cards can be developed within peer study groups or downloaded from the BRAIN Web site.

There are several methods commonly used to prepare for the ABCN written examination including independent study, completing CE workshops, attending presentations at professional meetings, working with a mentor, or participating in an organized peer study group. Many who have successfully passed the written examination have used more than one of these study methods to prepare for the examination.

The ABCN written examination is the type of test that lends itself to regular and systematic preparation over many months, instead of cramming the week before the exam. You should avoid waiting until the last minute to begin studying. Solo studying for the written examination might best begin by concentrating on review of the authoritative texts in neuropsychology and clinical neurology rather than browsing through recent journals. The *AACN Study Guide* contains a list of these important books, although it has been several years since this reading list has been updated. The BRAIN online peer study group recommends reading *Fundamentals of Human Neuropsychology* (Kolb & Whishaw, 2003), which they view as one of the best general review books. BRAIN also suggests reviewing *Clinical Neuropsychology* (Heilman & Valenstein, 2003) for its syndrome-based approach and *Neuroanatomy Through Clinical Cases* (Blumenfeld, 2002) as one of the best texts for reviewing clinical neuroanatomy. *Textbook of Clinical Neuropsychology* (Morgan & Ricker, 2008) is a more recent comprehensive book that covers clinically relevant, current knowledge about neurological disorders that are commonly encountered in clinical practice across the lifespan (there are 13 chapters devoted to pediatric topics).

Other self-study resources are available through the written exam Web page of the BRAIN study support group: http://www.cincinnatichildrens.org/svc/alpha/n/neurobehavioral/brain/written/default.htm. On this page, you can browse and download all of the written examination notes that have been prepared over the years by members of the BRAIN group. In addition, you can use all of the BRAIN group's electronic flash cards that were developed with the written examination in mind.

Practice written examination questions are also available through both the AACN and the BRAIN Web sites. The *AACN Study Guide* contains 30 practice multiple-choice questions that are intended to resemble actual written examination items in scope and depth. The BRAIN study group has developed a full-length mock written examination that attempts to be roughly equivalent to the ABCN exam in content. These two resources can provide a sense of what to expect from the written examination. The BRAIN group recommends using these questions to help guide study strategies by signaling areas of strength and weakness.

Individuals interested in becoming board certified might also find one of the ABCN board examination CE workshops useful, which, as mentioned earlier, are usually offered in conjunction with some of the national neuropsychology organization meetings. By understanding what is expected at each phase of the examination process and getting advice on how best to prepare for each component, you can help allay your anxiety as you proceed through the examination process. In addition, attendance of CE workshops covering topics in which one's knowledge base is less than optimal may also help in preparing for the written examination.

Candidates can also supplement their individual study by either working with a mentor, such as those available through the AACN mentorship program at no cost to the candidate, or by joining a peer study group, such as those organized through the BRAIN Web site. Since all AACN mentors are board certified, they have an understanding of the knowledge and skills it takes to successfully navigate all phases of the process, including the written examination. Mentors can recommend or assign readings covering the major content areas contained in the examination or, after engaging in discussions across a broad range of topics in neuropsychology and quizzing or probing the candidate's breadth of knowledge, mentors may help identify areas in which the candidate is lacking and needs remediation. Furthermore, by providing regularly scheduled meeting times for content review, mentors can help candidates stay on track to meet their projected time-frame goals for taking the examination.

Yet another way to prepare for the written examination is by joining a peer study group. Currently, going to the BRAIN Web site to become involved with a study group composed of individuals who are at similar stages in the board certification process is probably the best method for finding an appropriate peer study group. The BRAIN study support group recommends joining a small group of three to four people who meet each week via telephone conference call in the 14 to 16 weeks preceding completion of the written examination. Sample schedules for these study groups are provided on both the AACN and BRAIN Web sites and include topics such as basic and clinical neurosciences, clinical and behavioral neurology, neuropsychological assessment, and general clinical psychology (e.g., psychopathology, experimental design, statistics, history of psychology).

During the conference calls, a member may take responsibility for presenting an overview of the reading topic assigned for that week, and members may then discuss, clarify, and review some of the more difficult details to help solidify the information. The study groups typically have a mixture of pediatric and adult-oriented members to ensure exposure to expertise across the lifespan. BRAIN peer study groups are also effective insofar as they exert gentle peer pressure to make each member accountable for the weekly reading assignments, provide peer support and encouragement, and lessen the anxiety that may be associated with examination preparation.

Preparation for the ABFP Written Examination

Preparation should begin at least several months before the written examination is scheduled and involve an in-depth review of the knowledge base domains listed in Table 6.2. Studying for the written examination provides candidates the opportunity to consolidate information acquired during previous training and supervision, and master new information in areas with which they are less familiar. It is important not to overprepare in a single area, especially in an area of particular interest or expertise. Rather, because of the written examination's goal of assessing breadth of knowledge, candidates preparing for the written examination will do best to identify and concentrate on topic areas with which they are less familiar. Then, upon passing the written examination, candidates can focus their attention and study on the two areas of practice to which their practice samples are devoted.

Many candidates worry about the degree to which the written examination will survey relevant case law. The examination certainly includes questions about cases that are relevant to the specialty practice of forensic psychology broadly, as well as cases relevant to content of the various subspecialty areas (see Table 6.2). However, no test questions are focused simply on ascertaining whether the candidate can remember the name of a particular case. Rather, all test questions involving case law focus on the substantive issue, not the case name.

The ABFP written examination lends itself to regular and systematic preparation over many months instead of cramming the week before the written examination. You should avoid waiting until the last minute to start studying. Independent studying for the written examination may be best accomplished by concentrating on reviewing key texts in forensic psychology rather than by attending professional meetings or workshops, or reviewing professional periodicals. The ABFP Suggested Reading List for Written and Oral Examinations (see above) contains a list of key books, including *Evaluating Competencies: Forensic Assessments and Instruments* (Grisso, 2003), *Forensic Psychology* (Goldstein, 2003), *Principles of Forensic Mental Health Assessment* (Heilbrun, 2001), and *Psychological Evaluations for the Courts: A Handbook for Mental Health Professional and Lawyers* (Melton et al., 2007).[3]

Candidates can certainly seek to expand their breadth of forensic knowledge, prepare for the written examination, and accumulate many frequent-flier miles by traveling to CE workshops offered by the AAFP and other groups. Workshop attendance alone, however, is likely to be unsuccessful and expensive. Indeed, one of the authors has suggested to candidates who have adopted the "workshop approach" to examination preparation that the money and time spent on traveling to distant cities and registering for CE workshops would be better spent by holing up for a few days in a nice hotel in a resort near their home and reading authoritative texts and other related references. This latter approach, of course, requires a level of motivation and "stick-to-it-tiveness" that everyone does not have.

Despite the limitations noted previously, there are some CE workshops that may prove particularly valuable for candidates preparing for the written and oral examinations in forensic psychology. The AAFP board examination preparation workshops can be helpful insofar as they make clear what is expected at each phase of the examination process and provide advice on how best to prepare for each component. In addition, selectively attending CE workshops devoted to topics in which one's knowledge base is lacking may assist in remedying specific deficits.

Another way to prepare for the written examination is by organizing a peer study group composed of psychologists who are at the same stage of the process (i.e., are preparing to take the written examination). Although neither the ABFP nor AAFP organizes such groups, it is easy to enlist colleagues at AAFP-sponsored CE workshops, and advances in technology allow candidates in different states to work together toward their joint goals. In some study groups, members rotate responsibility for gathering readings and leading the discussion on a particular topic. Other groups function more like study cooperatives in which members share resources (e.g., chapter outlines and the like), and other groups serve primarily a support function. If a group is successfully established, it can continue to function for the members through the various stages of the examination process.

Finally, one-on-one supervision and mentoring can also be helpful in preparing for the written examination. Substantive issues can be addressed in the context of case supervision or more formally.

Summary

Although the board certification process requires a fair amount of time and commitment, most individuals who have gone through the process have found it to be a valuable experience that has substantively improved their professional knowledge and skills regardless of the outcome. Successful completion of ABPP board certification provides psychologists with not only legitimate recognition of demonstrated competence in their area of specialization but, in many cases, also tangible benefits, such as better job opportunities and financial rewards, as well as pronounced personal satisfaction.

Endnotes

1. The examination was also administered to six non-board-certified forensic psychologists who frequently practice in the forensic area. Their mean score of 80.0 was a little more than 1 standard deviation below the average score of the 53 board-certified forensic psychologists.
2. A CD that includes many of the legal cases in the reference list (*Key Legal Cases in Forensic Mental Health*; Connell, Conroy, & Witt, 2006) can be purchased from Professional Resource Press (www.prpress.com).
3. In the interest of full disclosure, the second author has contributed to and has a financial interest in at least some of these volumes.

Preparing the Practice Sample

Charme Sturkie Davidson, PhD, ABPP
Specialty in Counseling Psychology

Introduction

This chapter focuses on the preparation of the practice sample for board certification by the ABPP through one of its 13 separate boards. Given the differences in procedures of the different boards, this chapter is more of a prototype guideline than an outline of the specific steps that apply for each board. There is variability in what the specialty boards require in the practice sample, and the manual of the specific board should serve as a more focused guideline for the individual candidate. In addition, there is some difference in terminology used by the various boards. For the purposes of this chapter, the practice sample includes the professional self-study statement, the curricula vitae, and the work sample. Again, although terminology varies from board to board, this chapter should provide a good overview for the preparation of the practice sample.

The preparation of the practice sample as a part of undertaking board certification with the ABPP is an exceedingly valuable exercise that serves two significant functions. First, of course, is the obvious: The practice sample is the required second step in the three-step board certification process. Second, and far more subtle than the first function, is the fact that preparation of the practice sample lays the groundwork and sets the tone for the subsequent oral examination. In the course of preparing the practice sample, candidates begin preparing themselves for the oral examination by defining the specific content of a case(s) (in whatever form) and by actuating their own cognitive and emotional processes.

Two Options for Preparation of the Practice Sample

As candidates approach board certification in any specialty area they first consider the two options that may be available to them. Candidates who have been practicing and have been licensed for at least 2 years are eligible for board certification following the traditional process for submitting the practice sample—the curriculum vitae, the professional self-study statement, and the work sample. In some specialty areas, candidates who have been in the professional field for many years (the number depends on the particular area of board certification but the minimum is 15 years) and who are classified as senior clinicians can choose the senior option, if made available by their specialty board. Candidates who do not classify as senior clinicians may be asked to prepare a different type of practice sample for board certification. It should be noted that candidates who are seniors are not bound to pursuing board certification through the senior option and may also choose to submit the more traditional practice sample. Finally, it is important to underscore the point that in all cases, the oral examination is the same for senior and traditional candidates. It is only that practice sample that may be somewhat different.

Points to Consider as Candidates Approach Preparation of the Practice Sample

Several specialties require an audiotape or CD, videotape or DVD, or a typed transcript of the materials presented for the oral examination. Be sure to carefully review the specific requirements of the board to which you are applying. The material specified by the individual board should be created and collected during the preparation of the practice sample. Chapter 9 of this book discusses in detail how preparation of the practice sample can be an important first step toward a successful oral examination.

The evaluation of the practice sample is an event unto itself. However, within the oral examination, the practice sample will be used as a basis of discussion. It is important to be prepared to discuss the practice sample during the oral exam.

In some specialties candidates have 1 year after being admitted to candidacy to complete the practice sample; the candidate needs to check this with the particular board. When candidates encounter extenuating circumstances, they request an extension from the person on the specialty board who provides an initial review of the practice sample. This individual is the "practice sample coordinator." Such requests will be reviewed and the extension is often granted.

If allowed by the individual board, candidates may have a psychologist, certified by their particular board, review the practice sample as part of a mentoring process. It can also be very helpful to have a mentor assigned to guide the candidate through the entire process. The amount of guidance provided by the mentor varies from board to board. However, the practice sample is much too important to risk a submission without it having been scrutinized carefully. Mentors can be helpful in reminding applicants not to let identifying information slip through cracks and ensure that all personal references are carefully removed.

Preparation of the Practice Sample

The practice sample most often consists of the curriculum vitae, a professional self-study statement, and the work sample. Although different specialties may have different formats for the practice sample, the purpose and content of the practice sample are essentially the same across the boards. Figure 7.1 presents a chart for the preparation of the practice sample and specifies some of the differences between the senior and traditional options.

Purposes of the Practice Sample

Undertaking the practice sample begins a process of self-examination during which candidates make an objective evaluation of what led them to the

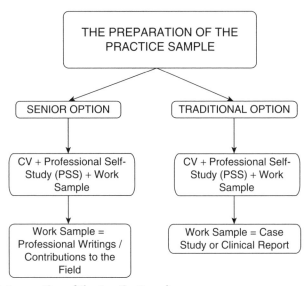

Figure 7.1 Preparation of the Practice Sample.

profession of psychology, how they have evolved in the course of working in the profession, and how they view themselves within the profession at the point when they undertook board certification. Preparing the practice sample brings candidates to an assessment of their own body of work and to a comparison of that body of work against current scientific bases, current diversity standards, and current ethical principles as each of these is incorporated in the profession at large.

The preparation of the practice sample requires an evaluation of one's work both implicitly and explicitly. Not only do candidates come to the preparation of the practice sample with their eyes on what they do, they also consider the self-reflective aspects of their work. During this process you may want to ask yourself the following questions:

- How do I anticipate the work that I do with a particular person or group?
- How do I prepare myself to do this work?
- How do I see myself relative to the person, group, or organization during the encounter?
- How do I evaluate how I have changed as a result of this encounter?
- How do I think about the potential outcomes for these interventions in the long and short term?

Although these questions need not be specifically answered in the practice sample, they should be considered in its preparation.

Let's look at the specific components of the practice sample. The purpose of the curriculum vitae is to provide reviewers and examiners a conventional, professional view of candidates. The curriculum vitae should follow the standard formulation of academic experience, professional history, awards and honors, as well as professional memberships. It should be emphasized that most applicants for board certification are not in academic settings and the vitae is not being evaluated by those standards. It should be regarded as a letter of introduction.

The professional self-study statement and the work sample set the foundation for the comprehensive experience of the examination. As a result, the preparation of the practice sample becomes more than a formulation of a professional self-study and the production of a work sample. There are two options available for the work sample (either the senior option or the standard practice work sample), and these are discussed in the sections that follow.

The Senior Option

The senior option provides an opportunity for senior clinicians to present their cumulative experience and professional work to complete the requirements for board certification. With this option, candidates can submit a portfolio consisting of published articles, book chapters, or books, innovative programs, documents prepared for accreditation (such as site visitors' reports), a practice summary, etc., instead of a traditional work sample, which is more case focused. Some specialties require a portfolio of written works such as reports of assessments, psychological examinations, organizational consultations, etc. To be sure that you are on the right track, you might want to seek consultation from the practice sample coordinator for the particular specialty. As mentioned previously, each specialty board has at least one individual designated as the practice sample coordinator.

When candidates choose the senior option, they write a professional self-study or professional statement. Use of the senior option does not eliminate the need for the professional self-study to provide a context for the candidate's

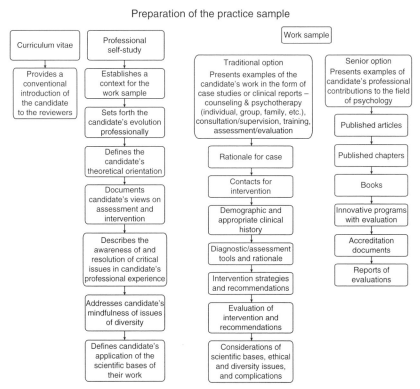

Figure 7.2 Practice Sample and Work Sample Preparation.

works. As in the traditional practice sample, candidates can provide evidence of their work in psychotherapy, consultation, supervision, training, management, or administration. Additionally, several boards suggest submission of a limited number of publications if they are relevant to professional practice.

Candidates will want to demonstrate consistency between the professional self-study and the portfolio. Just as in the case of the traditional practice sample, the professional self-study sets the groundwork for the materials presented in the portfolio in a connected and continuous manner.

A discussion of the traditional option for the practice sample will be presented shortly. However, you may want to examine Figures 7.2, 7.3, and 7.4 to help differentiate between the two options. In addition, they serve to further clarify the process.

The Professional Self Study

The professional self-study or professional statement is exactly what its title suggests: It is the document by which candidates explain and document their evolution as professionals, their views and beliefs about psychological

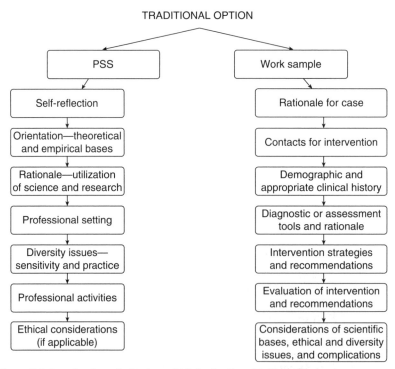

Figure 7.3 Practice Sample Options. PSS, Professional Self-study.

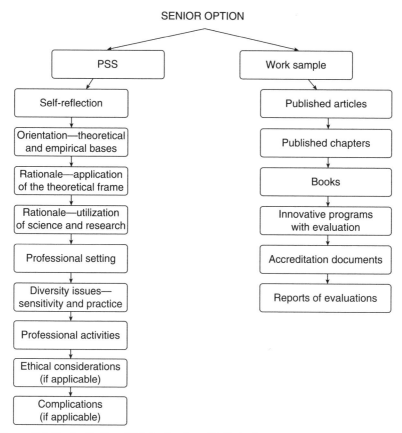

```
                          SENIOR OPTION


         ┌──────────────────┐          ┌──────────────────┐
         │       PSS        │          │   Work sample    │
         └──────────────────┘          └──────────────────┘
                  │                             │
     ┌─────────────────────────┐    ┌──────────────────────────┐
     │     Self-reflection     │    │    Published articles    │
     └─────────────────────────┘    └──────────────────────────┘
                  │                             │
     ┌─────────────────────────┐    ┌──────────────────────────┐
     │  Orientation—theoretical│    │    Published chapters    │
     │   and empirical bases   │    └──────────────────────────┘
     └─────────────────────────┘                │
                  │                  ┌──────────────────────────┐
     ┌─────────────────────────┐    │          Books           │
     │  Rationale—application  │    └──────────────────────────┘
     │ of the theoretical frame│                │
     └─────────────────────────┘    ┌──────────────────────────┐
                  │                  │   Innovative programs    │
     ┌─────────────────────────┐    │     with evaluation      │
     │   Rationale—utilization │    └──────────────────────────┘
     │ of science and research │                │
     └─────────────────────────┘    ┌──────────────────────────┐
                  │                  │  Accreditation documents │
     ┌─────────────────────────┐    └──────────────────────────┘
     │   Professional setting  │                │
     └─────────────────────────┘    ┌──────────────────────────┐
                  │                  │   Reports of evaluations │
     ┌─────────────────────────┐    └──────────────────────────┘
     │     Diversity issues—   │
     │  sensitivity and practice│
     └─────────────────────────┘
                  │
     ┌─────────────────────────┐
     │  Professional activities│
     └─────────────────────────┘
                  │
     ┌─────────────────────────┐
     │  Ethical considerations │
     │      (if applicable)    │
     └─────────────────────────┘
                  │
     ┌─────────────────────────┐
     │      Complications      │
     │      (if applicable)    │
     └─────────────────────────┘
```

Figure 7.4 Senior Option. PSS, Professional Self-study.

assessment and intervention, and their attunement to ethical, professional, and diversity issues. The professional self-study provides an avenue for candidates to look at what has informed their practice, what has shaped them developmentally as psychologists, the biases they bring to their work, and how they evaluate their work, among other things. The self-study is the vehicle through which candidates communicate who they are professionally and what they do. This professional statement informs the reviewers and examiners about the candidate in such a way that the reader obtains an image of the candidate that has been transferred to the written page.

In the course of writing a professional self-study statement, candidates define their evolution as psychologists by examining their major influences and setting forth the theoretical basis for their work. As they define themselves, candidates will likely invoke specific references (e.g. articles, books, individuals) that have influenced and informed their development. They might also cite specific academic, supervisory, or personal experiences that have led them to have the beliefs and skills that they bring to the certification process. The self-study statement clearly conveys how the candidates' educational, supervisory, therapeutic, or personal experiences have shaped their beliefs and practice as professional psychologists.

Candidates describe the theoretical and empirical bases for their assessment, intervention, consultation, supervision, training, management, or administrative practices. Here candidates will include a discussion of their professional, theoretical frameworks and the ways that theory and research have influenced them as professionals and in their practice. Candidates elaborate on the major themes in their theoretical stances. Candidates can use this opportunity to address how their theoretical model informs their attitudes and behaviors about diversity and how it affects their assessment and intervention practices. As candidates discuss their own theoretical and empirical development and orientation, they are encouraged to be mindful of and discuss the limitations of their chosen models.

Within the self-study document, candidates define their approaches to psychological assessment and intervention. Depending on the venues in which they work and on their specialty choice, candidates might articulate these approaches as they relate to consultation, supervision, and family, group, or individual psychotherapy. Specifically, in the professional self-study, candidates describe the professional activities in which they are currently engaged, including their practice (setting, types of clients, description of various roles in their practices) and professional activities locally, regionally, nationally and internationally; their continuing professional education; their long-term goals for their professional practices; and their reasons for undertaking board certification.

Candidates need to explain and document their views and beliefs about psychological assessment and intervention. Candidates should clarify the assessments and interventions they use and the reasons why they have chosen them.

Of particular significance in the self-study statement is the candidate's treatment of the issues of multiculturalism and diversity. Candidates need to demonstrate their awareness of and sensitivity to contextual issues and acknowledge the impact that issues of diversity have on both assessment and intervention. Diversity subsumes race, ethnicity, gender, age, sexual orientation, class, and religion; physical and psychological challenges; geographic region of birth and rearing, as well as current residence, linguistic facility, and history.

Candidates should also provide evidence for their utilization of and contribution to the scientific bases in the practice of psychology. While it is not expected that all candidates contribute to the scientific literature, candidates should discuss how scientific evidence informs their practices as they formulate and evaluate the work that they do. If applicable, candidates may describe their own clinical research and the ways that their research activities inform the professional practice of psychology.

Some specialty boards have different requirements for the specific content of the professional self-study. For instance, several specialties expect candidates to describe ethical challenges that they have encountered in their work, to discuss complex, professional interpersonal relationships that they have managed in their professional arenas, to define concerns that they have about the profession (locally, regionally, and nationally), and to verify that they have had no legal or ethical actions or judgments occur since they were admitted to candidacy. These issues might not be mandated in the professional self-study for any one specialty, but they will be expected in some formulation in the oral examination. Although the length varies from specialty to specialty, candidates are generally expected to present the professional self-study within the confines of an 8- to 10-page document, which includes bibliographical references. As with all required documentation is it important to review the guidelines for submission of all relevant documents specific to the specialty of interest.

The Standard Work Sample

For many candidates, the work sample (case presentation) involves the presentation of case material from the candidate's actual practice. As candidates begin to develop the body of work to be presented in the work sample, they should consider choosing a case that reflects the context and content of their particular professional practices. Obviously, in most cases candidates will have the option of presenting an applied case study with an individual, a group, a couple, or a family; a consultation with a supervisee or a business (for example, a law firm, hospital, or mental health center); a training model used with organizations, in classrooms, or in communities; a psychological assessment for legal or medical use; or a site visitor's report prepared for accreditation, to list a few examples. The case should be representative of the candidates' practice.

Again, different specialty boards have different expectations for the content and process of the work sample. Incumbent on the candidate is a through review of the specific instructions for the work sample set forth by the specialty board whose certification the candidate is pursuing. For instance, different specialty boards may have different limits on the length of the work sample.

Candidates are required to obtain a consent for release of information from the entity presented in the case, no matter what kind of case is submitted.

At the outset, candidates need to state the rationale for the case that they have chosen to use in the work sample. They should formulate the work sample in a manner relevant to their own professional purposes and theoretical orientations as well as to the content of the professional self-study. If candidates use models of psychological assessment such as standardized tests, they need to document the rationale for the testing procedures used and note the value and limitations of those tests from the perspective of diversity. If they do not use formal assessment instruments, they should provide a rationale for this practice.

When candidates use psychotherapy cases for the work sample, whether an intake interview or an ongoing case, they should establish the context for their assessment and treatment. They must present the clients(s) in such a fashion that will protect the client's or clients' personal identity, and set forth demographic information pertinent to the case. Candidates will need to describe presenting problems and symptoms and delineate any significant medical or personal histories of the client(s) including the developmental issues of the client(s) and the client's or clients' family. They will also need to elucidate the psychological history of the client(s). Finally, candidates should describe the history of the condition and its prior treatment.

Candidates must also formulate the assessment or diagnosis of the client's or clients' issue using standard diagnostic or descriptive procedures appropriate to their specialty. Candidates need to set forth potential and actual intervention strategies as recommendations for treatment. Then they should describe the course of their work with the client(s). Finally, they should evaluate their interventions with specific reference to the intervention that had been planned. Throughout this assessment and intervention, candidates must remain mindful of the impact of diversity and note the impact of diversity.

When candidates use a consultation or supervision case (regardless of the venue in which the consultation or supervision takes place), they need to define the context and history of the situation and designate the "client." In addition, they should formulate the consultation or supervision relative to the purpose of the consultation or supervision and in light of their own theoretical orientation. They must specifically describe their assessment of the case and their intervention in the case. They must be mindful of issues of ethics and diversity and should describe the evaluation of the intervention. If a third or fourth party has commissioned the report and is to be implementing the content and process of the intervention, the recommendations for treatment or change should be provided in the work sample.

Obviously, consultation and supervision occur in many ways and in many different settings, depending on the area of specialization. Candidates must consult the individual specialty boards to conform to the specific expectations and directions for preparing the practice samples.

When candidates present a training model, they need to delineate the context in which the training takes place and the rationale for the training. They must also state the purpose for the training and the desired outcomes, and formulate how they approached the training in terms of content and process as well as their personal preparation. Candidates must present their evaluation of the training with regard to its purpose and demonstrate their attunement to issues of diversity.

When candidates submit a report of an assessment or evaluation, they must present a case that is representative of their practice but sufficiently complex to demonstrate the candidates' breadth of professional and clinical proficiency. They must clearly state the reason for the referral and describe the purpose of the examination. The conceptual basis and rationale for selection of testing or other assessment procedures must be clearly evident. Assessment data should be reported and presented in a clear and well-organized format. The candidates must provide support for their conclusions and for their recommendations in the professional literature, with specific citations if appropriate. Relevant historical and medical risk factors need to be identified and integrated into the formulation of the report. Candidates also need to appropriately assess and incorporate any emotional or psychopathological factors into the report. An "original" clinical report is submitted, written in a clear, professional style, that has been tailored to the background and need of the identified primary consumer of the report. The report should conform to ethical standards and reflect an awareness of those standards. Candidates need to set forth treatment recommendations, including additional evaluative comments, that are substantive and well founded and that offer sufficient detail to foster their implementation. Interpretation of the results should be made in a way that demonstrates the candidates' knowledge and appreciation of the relationship between individual differences and social influences.

Generally, candidates submit three or four copies of their practice samples to the practice sample coordinator of the board through which the candidates are seeking board certification. Candidates must check with the specialty board to which the practice sample will be submitted to determine exactly how copies are to be transmitted and how many copies are to be submitted.

Evaluation of the Practice Sample

Each specialty board has its unique way of evaluating practice samples. As a result, candidates should review the examination manual for each board for the specific process. The model set forth here generally describes how practice samples are evaluated. When the practice sample coordinator receives the practice sample, reviewers are selected. For some specialties these reviewers will be the team that conducts the oral examination and for other specialties independent reviewers are used. In either case, teams of board-certified psychologists evaluate the practice samples. The team reviewing the practice sample may or may not be matched according to theoretical orientation or practice setting.

After the practice sample coordinator receives a candidate's practice sample and selects the reviewing and examining team, the practice sample coordinator sends the practice samples out for review. In most cases, the team has 30–45 days in which to evaluate the practice sample.

Each member of the team reads the practice sample and considers how it should be evaluated. Then the members of the team may or may not speak with each other (according to the specialty) before making a determination of the status of the practice sample. Reviewers rate the practice sample using those standards set forth in the specific instructions for preparing the practice sample by the particular specialty board. Just as candidates must be mindful of the scientific bases of their work, issues of diversity, and ethical concerns, reviewers must keep these issues in mind when performing the evaluation.

When reviewing the practice sample, the team looks for evidence that supports the candidate's theoretical approach to assessment and intervention, defines the specific training and experience that shaped the candidate's theoretical approach, and demonstrates the candidate's clinical proficiencies. Further, the team should have a clear description of the case(s) presented in a traditional work sample. The committee looks for the purpose of the assessment and intervention, the rationale for the assessment and intervention, the conclusions drawn from the assessment and intervention, and the risk factors involved in the assessment, intervention, and conclusions. The committee also looks for the ethical issues, if any, confronted in the assessment, intervention, and conclusions, the candidate's awareness of issues of diversity, and the treatment recommendations, as applicable, resulting from the assessment and intervention.

When reviewing practice samples submitted under the senior option, reviewers expect the professional self-study and the portfolio to be correlated and consistent in content and process. After the reviewers make their assessments of a practice sample they rate it. Again, the rating system used varies from board to board. They may rate it as acceptable, as acceptable with revisions, or as unacceptable, or simply pass or no pass.

If the practice sample is rated as acceptable, the candidate moves forward to the oral examination phase of the board certification process. In this case, the reviewers may prepare questions, which will likely be used during the oral examination. In some specialty areas, the practice sample may be rated as acceptable with revisions and can require either major or minor revisions. The reviewing team will inform the candidate of the team's specific concerns and in some cases the review team will continue to work with the candidate on revision of the practice sample until the team's concerns have been resolved. In these cases what is pertinent to this rating is that the candidate work with the original practice sample until it is found to be acceptable by the team of reviewers. Candidates may have a set time period in which to complete the revisions on the practice sample. When the practice sample is rated as acceptable, the candidate moves on to the oral examination (see Fig. 7.5).

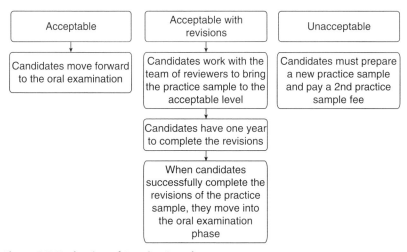

Figure 7.5 Evaluation of Practice Sample.

If the practice sample is rated as unacceptable, the candidate is informed of the problems with the practice sample. The candidate essentially starts the practice-sample phase of the board certification process anew, because the candidate must prepare another, different practice sample to continue moving forward. Frequently, when candidates' practice samples have been rated as unacceptable, they are able to prepare the second practice sample efficiently, based on the knowledge and skill that they acquired in preparation and evaluation of the first practice sample. When the second practice sample is completed, a different reviewing team evaluates the additional practice sample. When the candidate achieves an acceptable rating on the practice sample, the candidate moves to the oral-examination phase of board certification. Figure 7.5 presents the various outcomes and the corresponding processes.

Summary

The practice sample is an extremely important part of the ABPP exam for all specialty boards. Many specialty boards offer an opportunity for professional psychologists with greater than 15 years of experience to submit an alternative sample of their contributions or work, allowing for greater flexibility than the standard clinical case. It is important to remember that the nature of the sample may vary from specialty to specialty. Candidates should carefully follow the guidelines for the specific board to which they are applying.

Acknowledgments

My special thanks and gratitude is extended to Evelyn Collete Sadowski for her generous help with the figures displayed in this chapter.

Working With a Board-Certified Mentor in the Specialty

Joseph E. Talley, PhD, ABPP
Specialties in Clinical and
Counseling Psychology

Introduction

In the process of becoming board certified by the ABPP, a candidate may request to be assigned to or elect to find a mentor. Having a mentor is not essential, but is something that many candidates find helpful. There is no reason to assume that you will not do well without having a formal mentor and instead relying on the information available on the ABPP Web site and asking various people within the ABPP who are qualified to answer your questions. In addition, it should be understood that having a mentor does not give you access to any special knowledge or enhance your desirability as a candidate in any way. On the other hand, many candidates like the support and guidance that a mentor can provide. If you want to consult primarily with one person throughout the entire process, a mentor may be useful.

The method and means of mentoring vary from specialty to specialty, just as the process has some variations from specialty to specialty. There may also be some variation in the level of supervision and support that is acceptable during mentoring. The mentor may provide advice on navigating the overall process step by step, including guidance in getting the appropriate documents sent for the credentials review phase and suggestions of how to best prepare for the oral examination. The mentor may also pass along some wisdom and encouraging ideas to assist in keeping the process in perspective. Mentors from some specialty areas may review practice samples and make suggestions, whereas other specialty areas discourage or do not permit this function.

Finding a Mentor

You may wonder, "How should I ask for a mentor?" The methods of finding a mentor vary. Many candidates use a more informal selection process and ask a board-certified specialist whom they already know or one who works with them if the specialist will assist them through the process. Both parties must then clarify the type of assistance that the candidate wants and what that specialist can provide. Sometimes candidates will ask colleagues to recommend a board-certified specialist in their area who might be willing to consider mentoring them. The word "mentoring" may not even be used in this informal process. The words "guide" or "assist" could be used equally well in an informal arrangement. It is best that the mentor not be a close friend or colleague, since that relationship may make it difficult for the mentor to identify areas needing work or focus. The candidate might also discount words of praise or encouragement as having been made because of the friendship.

To begin a more formal process, the word "mentor" should be used. The first step is to read the ABPP specialty board Web site that you are most interested in and determine if it provides information on how mentoring is set up within that specialty.

If you have difficulty finding a mentor, the names and contact information for the current president of that specialty's academy and the contact information for that specialty's examining board president can be obtained from the ABPP central office. Mentoring is often coordinated through the specialty academy. Currently, the president of the academy coordinates the assignment in a number of specialty areas—for example, with Cognitive-Behavioral Psychology and with Counseling Psychology. The president of the examining board of the specialty might be contacted for information not obtained through the ABPP central office, Web sites, or an academy president.

The Academy of Clinical Neuropsychology has a very well-developed mentoring program. They have concluded that a mentor can be of considerable benefit to candidates and encourage candidates to e-mail the coordinator of mentoring. Their BRAIN Web site (see Chapter 6 for more information) has been reported to be very helpful with this process.

In Rehabilitation Psychology all candidates are strongly encouraged to use a mentor, and the secretary of the examining board assigns a mentor to each candidate. Mentors are usually members of their academy and may be trained to do this function, thus ensuring more uniformity.

Several specialty groups track the progress of candidates and receive periodic reports from mentors on a candidate's progress. In addition, some groups offer workshops for their candidates at various conferences. There is considerable variation among the specialty areas. For example, Rehabilitation Psychology has a more organized mentoring program than that of many other specialties, although other specialties may offer workshops as well. The Academy of Clinical Child and Adolescent Psychology provides mentoring when a request is received through the ABPP central office. However, they have not yet developed any protocol for this process. For the specialty of School Psychology, after an application has been received by the ABPP central office, the director of mentoring assigns a mentor who is a fellow of the academy. This person assists in and explains each step of the process to provide a seamless transition from one step to the next. The mentor will answer questions along the way, review practice samples, and provide advice for the oral exam.

Mentoring Guidelines

Several guidelines developed by specialties are presented here to illustrate the mentoring process. However, as mentioned earlier, the process is not uniform across all specialty areas, and you should consult with the individual specialty area for specific information. The American Board of Couples and Family Psychology (ABCFP) uses the following mentoring guidelines:

Eligibility as a Mentor

1. Any ABPP board-certified specialist in the ABCFP is eligible to mentor candidates.
2. Members of the ABCFP board of directors may function as mentors, except for the president.
3. The mentor of a candidate may not be involved with credentials review, the practice sample review, the examination committee, or any other part of the evaluation or appeals process of the particular mentee.

Coordination of Mentors

1. The president-elect of the academy will serve as coordinator of the mentoring committee.

Obtaining a Mentor

1. All candidates shall be notified that they may request a mentor once they have requested an application for board certification in couple and family psychology.
2. The request for a mentor should be made to the coordinator, who shall recommend a mentor and appoint said person, if agreed upon.
3. The mentor shall contact the candidate to offer his or her assistance.
4. Nothing in these guidelines should be construed as prohibiting a candidate from obtaining his or her own mentor. In such a case, the mentor shall notify the coordinator of his or her selection immediately.

The Mentor's Role

1. To provide encouragement
2. To clarify questions regarding the requirements for the work samples
3. To emphasize the high quality required of the videotapes or DVDs
4. To provide guidance if requested on broad issues regarding the practice samples and exam process (for example, mentors may assist a candidate by identifying gaps in knowledge and make recommendations for further reading)
5. Mentors will not provide specific comments on the adequacy of a candidate's practice samples.
6. Mentors will not speak to the members of the examination committee about the candidate.
7. Mentors will not provide feedback to the candidate on the examination.
8. At a candidate's request, a mentor may discuss with the candidate the feedback the candidate received from the examination committee. However, he or she may not seek to have a "fail" decision reversed or purport to be speaking officially for ABCFP or ABPP.
9. Having a mentor does not in any way guarantee that the candidate's practice samples will be approved, nor will it increase his or her chances of passing the exam. All decisions are made objectively by the committee on the sole bases of the submissions and the performances on the examination.
10. Mentors are expected to stay abreast of current changes in expectations of the ABCFP and its examining committees.
11. Mentors should be in contact with the coordinator if they have any questions or concerns.
12. Mentors in this context are not permitted to charge a fee for their service.

As another example, the mentoring guidelines for the American Academy of Clinical Psychology (AACP) are as follows:

1. Mentors will advise those mentored regarding the application and examination processes, including qualifications, the preparation of work samples, and preparation for the oral examination. Those mentored may be new applicants or those who have taken but not passed the examination, and may be applicants for either the regular or the "senior" examination.

2. After the applicant contacts the AACP president to request a mentor, a mentor is assigned by the AACP mentoring coordinator. The mentor will contact the applicant to offer his or her services.

3. Contact with mentors will usually be through telephone or e-mail. Face-to-face meetings may occur occasionally, if geographically feasible, but the relationship is an advising rather than a teaching relationship, and this mentoring can almost always be accomplished through other means than face to face. There is no limit to the number of contacts, as long as both parties are willing and feel that the contacts are still useful.

4. Guidance to those mentored may include explanations, tailored to the needs of each applicant, of the philosophy, structure, and rationale for the board certification processes, as well as explanation of the viewpoint and expectations of examiners. These explanations will help those being mentored to better prepare their personal statements and work samples, to know how to describe their practice orientation and procedures, and to be prepared to answer questions about their work samples and about ethical issues in the examination. It is hoped that the comments and advice of mentors will serve to put the examination in an appropriate context and allay any unnecessary anxiety on the part of applicants.

5. Mentors may read professional statements, if requested, but comments will be limited to matters of incompleteness or ambiguity. Mentors will not view, read, or give *specific* advice regarding the content of any written or recorded examination materials. Advice will be limited to information that helps the applicant to understand what is needed for the examination process and how his or her materials may be viewed by examiners, so the applicant will be able to respond to the examination process to the best of his or her own ability.

6. Mentors may raise questions about possible deficits in the applicant's professional knowledge and skills, but mentors do not tutor applicants or take on the task of upgrading the knowledge and skills of applicants, except by occasionally recommending readings, courses, and supervision that might be helpful and that are carried out without the involvement of the mentor.

7. Mentors do not certify anyone's readiness to take the examination or speculate on an applicant's likelihood of passing the examination. If they choose to, mentors may offer comments on an applicant's professional strengths and weaknesses, if requested. Comments and advice of mentors are not communicated to the ABCP or to examiners, have no bearing on the examination outcome, and may not be used to appeal an examination outcome.

8. Applicants are reminded that, periodically, members of the AACP and of the American Board of Clinical Psychology offer workshops, at psychology conventions or otherwise, describing and explaining board certification processes and answering all questions about these processes, just as a mentor would.

In addition to having a mentor, getting together with other candidates every couple of weeks for lunch and discussion can provide support and motivation. It is also a way to learn from peers about materials they have read and found helpful.

Finally, the benefits of having a mentor often extend well beyond the candidacy process. A mentor will frequently introduce the former candidate and now board-certified colleague to other board-certified specialists, thus beginning a networking process. These meetings may result in the newly board-certified specialist being asked to be a work sample reviewer or examiner for an upcoming candidate. After assisting in the work sample review a few times, it is not uncommon to be asked to serve on a committee and then to be a candidate for an office. Throughout these activities the board-certified specialist meets and talks with new colleagues from around the country who share similar interests. These relationships can become important sources of information on matters of specialty practice and practice in a particular context. Eventually, this group of colleagues can become a primary professional reference group and, over the years, the closest of friends.

Summary

The value of mentors may rest in the warm advice and wisdom they share through the process. One mentor was known to say, "Just have fun with it." Receiving this type of advice from a seasoned mentor can be just what one needs to hear in order to benefit fully from the collegial exchange that occurs as part of the ABPP examination. Ultimately, many board-certified specialists report the exam to be an enjoyable day spent comfortably talking with new colleagues while taking the opportunity to share their enthusiasm for their professional work.

How to Prepare for the
Oral Exam

*Florence W. Kaslow, PhD, ABPP
Specialties in Clinical, Couple and
Family, and Forensic Psychology*

Introduction

This chapter is intended to welcome you to the world of the ABPP oral exam and to clarify what it entails. It is important to point out that the actual process may vary somewhat across the 13 specialty boards; when possible, some of these differences will be discussed. The chapter is based on my experience as an examiner over the past 30 years for the Forensic, Clinical, and Couples and Family Psychology Boards, and from serving as a workshop leader training examiners for the American Board of Couples and Family Psychology. I have also had many conversations with examiners from other specialties over the years to augment my own experience with oral examinations in my specialty areas.

The information provided in this chapter is structured in such a way as to provide advice and discuss the initial steps in the process so that you will increase the likelihood of a successful oral examination. Whereas other chapters also cover these preliminary steps in the process, such as preparing a practice sample, they are discussed here specifically in terms of how to maximize successful completion of the oral examination. The sections that follow describe each of these steps.

Acquire a Mentor

Although a separate chapter has been devoted to this topic (Chapter 8), it is important to underscore both the utility and benefits of acquiring a mentor to provide guidance in the process of preparing for the exam. Many boards and their corresponding academies have a system for providing the candidate with a mentor. Some boards also permit the candidate to select and approach directly someone who is board certified in the specialty and with whom they would like to work as a mentor. If this route is chosen, the appropriate person, usually the chairperson of the specialty's mentor committee, or the chairperson of the specialty board, should be notified. This helps to ensure the integrity and transparency of the process. The mentor can work with the candidate and supply more specific information than either the particular specialty board manual or this chapter will offer. Working closely with a good mentor is often advisable and enlightening, as both mentors and applicants can learn from this collaborative relationship.

For example, in couple and family psychology, I occasionally find a candidate I am mentoring to have a relatively weak background in formal assessment procedures to use in making dynamic family diagnoses. As another example, I may be precepting a candidate who has been rigorously trained and then continues to adhere to one or two prominent theoretical models, but whose knowledge base does not encompass any familiarity with other important philosophic and theoretical schools with which we expect a competent couple and family psychologist to be conversant. In both cases, I would advise the candidate on ways to expand his or her knowledge base or skills in the area(s) in which gaps are identified.

Advice on Exam Preparation

The materials submitted prior to your exam and discussed in more detail in Chapter 7 represent your first introduction to specialty examination. The degree of professionalism, comprehensiveness, and neatness in presentation will create an impression of the quality of your work. We all know how important first impressions can be. Thus, it is important to remember that a top-quality audio- or videotape or DVD in your practice sample that is easily reviewable and audible to the examiners will help set the stage for a high-quality examination. All written materials should be submitted in booklet or compendium form and well prepared in content and style so that examination chairs or examiners can read them carefully and transport them easily to the exam site. Be certain the materials you submit are representative of the work you are actually doing currently and that you are proud to submit them. Sloppy or poorly written materials that may be unrepresentative of your day-to-day work significantly detract from professionalism.

Advice on Submitting the Practice Sample

Assessment and intervention competencies are partially evaluated from the submitted samples of the candidate's practice, which are discussed and evaluated during the oral examination. Although advice on how to submit the practice sample is described in extensive detail in Chapter 7, there are some important points to remember about submission of your written documents, as it relates to the oral exam.

Each audio- or videotape or DVD sample should be approximately 50 minutes in length. Specialty boards requiring two practice samples expect one depicting an unrehearsed psychological assessment effort and the other showing an unrehearsed intervention effort. Each should illustrate the candidate's typical clinical practice during the year prior to submission. Specific requirements regarding which session in a series should be recorded vary among different specialties. Recordings are usually required to represent one continuous, unedited session and should display visible and audible interactions between the candidate and the person receiving services. Good audio quality is essential and best obtained by the use of lapel microphones for all individuals in the video, or a strong area microphone. There may be specifications for the preferred format required in various specialties, such as whether the audio or video samples must be in digital format. An important part of preparing the practice sample is confirming that the sample meets these specifications. Check with the specialty board to which you are applying about the format and technology they prefer or require, and arrange to use the very best equipment, and a technician if needed.

During the examination, candidates are often asked, "How did you handle the issue of confidentiality with your client when you decided to submit client material as part of your practice samples?" It is important to remember the following guidelines concerning client consent. When using information from their records and clinical progress, as well as any audio or video images, it is important to obtain client or patient consent for the use of these materials during the oral exam. Consent forms should be obtained and a copy of the signed consent form brought to the oral exam in a sealed envelope for placement in the candidate's examination file in the ABPP central office. When one is seeing multiple clients, remember to obtain consent from all relevant persons. This occurs frequently in many specialties, such as in a couple and family, group psychology, cognitive and behavioral skills training groups, rehabilitation psychology groups, organizational consultations, or clinical health support groups.

For many boards, documents and contextual statements of between 1,000 and 1,500 words are required as part of the practice sample, which delineate the following:

1. The rationale for the procedures used
2. A reflective comment on the candidate's own behavior in the sample session
3. Commentary on relevant events for the candidate or client subsequent to the taped sample
4. Anything specialty specific that an individual specialty board requires as part of assessment or intervention documentation

Although Chapter 7 describes the content preparation of the practice sample in more detail, the technical suggestions that follow are likely to result in an enhanced oral examination experience.

Practice Sample Supporting Documentation

Video Requirements and Techniques

1. Videos should clearly show the face and body of the therapist as well as each client present in the session. This is particularly important when parent–child, couples, family, or group therapy sessions are being taped. It is also essential when a session consulting to an organization is the focus. (In some cases, two or more cameras may be necessary to show everyone.)
2. Cameras should not be pointed at lamps, bright lights, or sunny windows, which shut down the camera aperture and make film quality too dark for effective and easy viewing.
3. Provide lapel microphones or strong area microphones for each person present, including the therapist, in order to easily pick up variances in voice tone and diction on the tape.
4. Arrange chairs for all clients and do a "dry run" with the camera with friends or colleagues to ensure that all chairs and persons will be visible in the camera range and that each microphone is recording voices distinctly. **Do not assume anything** about cameras, microphones, etc. without a rehearsal to check out everything! Check all cables, power cords, and even adapter plugs (with three prongs) to be certain all equipment will operate properly before your clients or patients arrive.
5. It may be necessary to rent equipment and/or hire a videographer if you need to submit a video and your work site does not have the technology, or if you are in a solo or small independent practice. Over the long run, it should be worth the investment.

Finally, candidates are encouraged to carefully select practice samples that reflect their areas of competence and display their interactive style. No session is expected to be perfect in execution or results.

Assessment Sample Content In my experience as an examiner in several specialty areas, I have found it helpful in the oral examination to have the following supplementary and contextual information easily available:

- Dates of contacts with patients (individual, couple, family, group members)
- Non-identifying descriptive information
- Presenting problem or issue
- Brief history
- Rationale for procedures used
- Copies of all raw data
- Formulation and discussion of the problem
- A reflective comment on the candidate's own behavior in the session
- A copy of the full professional, written report that captures any patient's diagnoses, treatment, and recommendations
- Where standardized assessment instruments are used, the candidate should have a thorough knowledge of the construction, administration, and interpretation of each assessment instrument or method used.

Intervention Sample Content With regard to an intervention practice sample, it is helpful for examiners to have the following available:

- Contact dates
- Session number in total sequence
- Non-identifying descriptive information
- Presenting problem(s)
- Diagnostic formulation
- Brief history
- Formulation and discussion of the problem(s)
- Rationale for interventions used
- Goals for present intervention(s)
- A reflective comment on the candidate's own behavior in the session

Advice on Preparing a "Philosophy of Practice" Statement

If a specialty board requires a professional self-study statement of your personal philosophy of practice, assume that the examination committee members will read it carefully. Part of the examination will involve an evaluation of whether or not the philosophy or theories that you elucidate and your stated areas of competence are reflected in and consistent with your practice samples. Therefore, you will want to make statements that you can back up and demonstrate in your answers to questions during the course of the exam. Be prepared to discuss your philosophy of practice and how this philosophy is actually manifested in what you do.

In addition, most boards require that the candidate describe in the professional statement his or her professional training, experience, and identity to augment the facts provided in the application form. This statement should illuminate the applicant's specific training and background in the specialty area. Writing this statement provides the opportunity for the candidate to communicate with the committee who he or she is professionally and his or her self-definition and identity, and may serve as a basis for some of the discussion in the opening portion of the oral examination.

It is each candidate's responsibility to write a statement capturing his or her theoretical orientation and to articulate how this orientation is translated into his or her practice. Further, the professional statement should encompass a description of the full scope of the candidate's professional activities beyond employment, such as involvement in professional organizations and in the community. In addition to being prepared to discuss your current career and professional interests and activities, the philosophy that informs your practice, and your practice samples, you should be conversant with the major current theories, issues, and trends in your psychology specialty and in the broader field that affects all psychologists.

For example, two important issues affecting all professional training and education programs in recent years, as well as all APA and ABPP policies and standards, have been competency-based education and practice (see Chapter 3), including competence in multicultural and diversity issues. Therefore, it is advisable to prepare discussion of how these issues have influenced the way you conducted an assessment or developed an intervention and the extent to which diversity and multicultural factors impact the sample of professional work being discussed. In some cases, examiners have asked candidates to explain how they might have made an assessment and or treatment decision differently if the patient were of a different cultural or ethnic background. For example, one possible situation in which such a question might be asked might occur during a clinical, child clinical, couple and family, or cognitive-behavioral exam, if the clinician is working with a white parent who is dealing with an adolescent daughter with emotional and behavioral difficulties. In such a case, depending on the other information provided in the preparation materials, an interviewer might ask how cultural and family factors might affect the case differently in a Latin, Japanese, Mormon, or Muslim family. While no one is ever expected to have a full breadth of all possible multicultural and diversity-based knowledge at their fingertips, it is extremely important for board-certified specialists to embrace the importance of multicultural factors in their work. The integration of multicultural and individual diversity factors throughout all professional functions and activities is considered a required competency across all specialties. Some demonstration of how such factors impact your practice will always be a topic to anticipate in any oral examination.

Advice on Staying Current

Many of us encourage those preparing for their oral examination to read, at a minimum, the recent issues of *Monitor* and the *American Psychologist*, on the broad field of psychology, plus the one or two most important journal series of the prior year in their specialty. While this may sound somewhat tedious, many board-certified specialists have reported that it was one of the most enjoyable aspects of preparation, because it provided them with an opportunity to review what they already knew, and to refresh and update their knowledge base. Moreover, I have heard more than once that becoming aware of new scholarly viewpoints or scientific findings resulted in challenging the specialist with new ideas and additional strategies to integrate into their work. Most of us who conduct examinations would say that the overwhelming number of psychologists who sit for a board certification exam report that the process helped them to grow professionally.

As exam day approaches, remember that you have passed through each stage of your training successfully to reach this point, including educational comprehensive exams, theses defenses, and the state licensing and national exam. You are successful at what you do and find your profession rewarding. As in most endeavors, this is an opportunity to discuss what you do. If it doesn't result in a full pass, you can analyze why this happened, and try again. Common-sense health advice, such as getting a good night's sleep the night before the exam and allowing extra time for any required travel to the exam site is likely to contribute to a sense of comfort and confidence and to decrease anxiety.

Advice on the Oral Examination: What to Expect

Finally, after what may have seemed like a very long wait, oral exam (OE) day arrives. The ABPP expectation is that throughout the examination process, the climate to be established between the candidate and the examiners should be a collegial, peer relationship in which the candidate is considered and treated as a mature, professional psychologist. The presumption is that the large majority of candidates will pass. Every attempt will be made to create a favorable examination situation in which the candidate is able to demonstrate his or her competencies. If asked, many board certified specialists would say that exam day turned out to be challenging, interesting, stimulating, satisfying, and valuable. Many decide that they will join the specialty board's respective academy if they do pass, and that someday they would like to be examiners for their own board.

Most, if not all, of the specialty boards try to ensure as much standardization of the examination process as possible. One way of doing this has been that most boards have established oral examination day schedules. A general pacing and sequencing of topics is followed to reduce to a minimum the possibility that candidates will receive differential treatment from different committees throughout the country.

Nonetheless, within each segment of the exam, there is room for variation in the time allotted for each topical segment, as modifications are made according to the judgment of the examination committee on what needs coverage. Relevant topics for discussion may be interwoven throughout, whenever and wherever deemed pertinent. A topic may receive cursory attention in its time slot on the schedule if it has been sufficiently covered elsewhere, or expanded beyond the suggested time limits if it has been glossed over previously.

Sample Summary Schedule of Examination

Any consecutive 4-hour time period can be used for the exam by mutual agreement of the candidate and committee, if it adheres to an approximation of the schedule presented in Table 9.1, at least for the Clinical Board and the Couple and Family Boards. This schedule is predicated on the assumption that the examiners have viewed the videotapes and reviewed all the written materials **in advance**.

Variations from this type of schedule may be minimal to significant for other specialty boards. For example, some specialty boards such as Clinical Health and Counseling use a "stationed examination" approach, in which the

Table 9.1 *Sample Summary Schedule of Examination*

Activity	Time Period	Minutes
Committee meets, organizes	9:00–9:15	15
Chairperson greets candidate, introductions. Procedures are described. Collegial nature of exam emphasized	9:15–9:30	15
Focus on professional statement and practice samples	9:30–11:15	105
Break	11:15–11:30	15
Focus on ethical and legal issues	11:30–12:00	30
Exam wrap-up, discussion, questions, any further information candidate may wish to provide	12:00–12:30	30
Return practice samples to candidate. Committee votes and writes report	12:30–1:00	30

candidate meets with various teams of examiners who represent different areas or stations to be examined—i.e., assessment, interventions, or ethics. The Cognitive and Behavioral Board devotes a portion of its exam to having the candidate consult with a live ("in vivo") client or supervisor. These particulars should be elucidated in each specialty board manual and should be the first resource consulted if you have any questions. Your mentor might be the second and the ABPP central office the third resources.

Advice Concerning the Ethics Portion of the Oral Exam

To enable a degree of standardization in the ethics portion of the examination, a file of prepared vignettes is maintained for each specialty and updated periodically by each specialty board. Although the specific procedure regarding evaluation of ethics competencies may vary from board to board, often one vignette is selected on a random basis for each exam and sent to the examination chairperson, who then distributes it to the examiners. By then the candidate will also likely have submitted, along with the professional statement, an ethics quandary or issue to discuss from his or her own professional experience.

During the ethics portion of the examination, many of the specialty boards give the candidate a standardized vignette to read quietly (and privately) and then return to discuss. The examining committee does not expect that a "right" answer will be given, but rather hopes the candidate will offer relevant options and demonstrate the ability to weigh them thoughtfully in light of the APA ethics principles and statutes. The candidate may be expected to discuss his or her own vignette in the same manner and spirit. This is the approach used by the Clinical, and Couple and Family Boards. Other boards may use written responses to a vignette or omit the use of a candidate-generated ethics vignette.

General questions on ethics may emerge at any time during the exam in regard to the case. All candidates are expected to be conversant with the APA Code of Ethics and its relevance to their professional activities.

At the end of the examination, both the examiners' and candidate's vignettes will be collected for return to the ABPP central office. Each vignette's use is tracked so that in the event of a candidate's failure, a new vignette will be used for the re-examination. Both examiners and candidates must treat the vignettes as confidential.

Summary

In light of the increasing number of theoretical positions and specialized intervention processes and techniques developing within some of the specialty areas, the candidate may anticipate a committee with examiners who share the candidate's broad theoretical orientation but who may not all have had wide experience with his or her particular foci, approach, or setting. Thus, the candidate should be prepared to discuss his or her areas of focus with a minimum of technical jargon so as to easily communicate with committee members who may have had less exposure than the candidate to a particular area of the candidate's practice.

At the end of the examination, the candidate is thanked for attending the exam and told that he or she will be notified by the executive officer of the ABPP regarding the decision on his or her status. This usually occurs within a month of the exam's completion.

The examination is a confidential and professional activity. No examiner may disclose what he or she has learned about the candidate before or during the examination, except in the official report to the Board of Trustees of the ABPP.

All communications concerning the results of the examination are faxed to the executive office of the ABPP by the chair of the examination committee as soon as possible after the conclusion of the exam. The committee, through the chairperson, sends its recommendation of a pass or fail decision, based on numerical scorings of the various segments of the exam, along with feedback that should be provided to the candidate. *It is not appropriate for a candidate to communicate with any examiner about the outcome of the examination.* If an examiner should receive a letter from a candidate, it should be forwarded to the executive officer of the ABPP via the committee chair.

The Oral Exam Experience

Virginia DeRoma, PhD, ABPP
*Specialty in Clinical Child and
Adolescent Psychology*

Introduction

This chapter is designed to provide a firsthand account of undertaking the oral examination. As such, it is written from the viewpoint of a candidate who has recently completed a successful exam experience. To help you navigate the process of the oral exam, the chapter discusses 10 challenges that candidates may encounter during the ABPP examination experience and provides advice on ways to meet each challenge. The challenges presented relate to the competency assessment forwarded by the examination process itself.

The demands introduced in this chapter begin with a focus on the importance of self-review, which might be conceptualized as the process of setting forth a brief, professional autobiography (any chapter of which might be perused closely by the panel). Challenges related to assessment, conceptualization of the case, incorporation of multiple theoretical perspectives, and treatment-technique selection all refer to demands inherent in the process of understanding the problem and treatment planning. Challenges found in selecting treatment techniques, informing the examiners about the treatment, and being prepared to discuss measures of change are more closely tied to the process of intervention and monitoring of outcome.

The chapter closes with an introduction to supervision, teaching, and consultation challenges, which address how we bridge our work with others for the sake of improving client or organizational welfare.

Finding Your Philosophical Exam Voice

The literature has documented the negative consequences of long delays for appointments following intakes when commitment of clients might be high (Manthei, 1996; May, 1991; Reitzel et al., 2006). Similarly, the immediacy with which you become focused on preparing for the exam might relate to the degree of positive affect with which you approach the task of preparation. While it may feel like the time between submission of your samples and the oral exam is short, you might also consider this short time lapse to be just what you need to stay motivated. In fact, you might think of your accomplishment in passing the written and observed portions of your assessment and treatment tapes (where applicable) as a gift that you have committed to opening up and using, rather than shelving. This gift is a journey into validating and elaborating on your professional self-identification. Given the association between self-efficacy and effectiveness with tasks, preparing early for this exam will make the difference between good showmanship and self-growth. Preparation will enable you to appreciate the largest gains through this examination. The exam process is an opportunity to enact, in a formal way, the philosophy that we live in our teaching and practicing careers—that growth is fostered through challenge. You must define the philosophy with which to approach the oral exam process. Philosophies associated with a relaxed, but responsible, approach to the oral exam include the following:

- I am fortunate to have a team of qualified professionals to help me reflect on my practice.
- I enjoy participating in processes that help bring higher definition to standards of practice.
- The process of requesting opinions on my work underscores my value for feedback and learning.
- There are experiential benefits to being evaluated that can help me to better appreciate and adopt the perspective of clients.
- The examiners are eager for me to display the competencies necessary to become credentialed and to welcome me as a board-certified colleague.

Avoid adopting the following perspectives:

- A candidate is incompetent until found competent by the panel.
- Anxiety can be impairing (remember that a little anxiety can be performance enhancing).
- The panel will try to ask trick questions, including something I know nothing about.

- This is a friendly process in which everyone passes.
- I will suffer through this until it ends.

Emphasis on the realistically positive and an internal locus of control can be helpful. These philosophies help to set up the challenges that follow as those we welcome instead of those we dread.

Challenge 1: Clarifying the Threat

Preparation for the oral exam can be conceptualized as two tasks. The first is articulating the processes that you engage in as a competent clinician. The second process involves changing. While your continuing-education, supervisory, and other professional experiences have likely continually shaped you as a professional, they were likely less evaluative of your holistic approach to the work. The evaluative element of this process can feel threatening. However, the panel of evaluators is a group of your peers, who want to confirm that your approach to assessment and treatment is responsible. Toward that end, your examiners will likely ask you about your philosophy and approach to practice, but in the context of an "uncovering" process, rather than attempting to trip you up or intentionally search for weaknesses. To the extent that you have volunteered for the process of having your competence evaluated, you have control over the threats that may loom large to you. Anxiety is likely the largest self-imposed threat that you face. The best remedy for anxiety is an informed exposure to the feared situation. Some of the challenges described in the sections that follow are accompanied by lists of the types of questions you may encounter from your examination panel. Others include questions that you may wish to consider prior to the exam. This chapter is not designed to inform you of the specific questions that will be asked. It is also important to note that the exam experience may vary among different specialties.

Challenge 2: Discerning Your Audience

Some panels begin the oral examination experience with an introduction of the panel members and their background and history. This can serve as a point of professional contact in a social context. It also presents an opportunity for you to identify the foundations of training and practice of your audience. Similar to learning the needs of students you teach or professionals to whom you are presenting at a conference, this information can be very valuable. You already share common ground, in that the panel members selected have competencies in the area in which you are seeking certification. Consider the following :

- Experience in an area similar to your case suggests that less explanation may be necessary at times.
- Past roles of the panel provide clues to the areas of interest and line of exam questioning.
- Their presentation will suggest a preferred style of communication, to which you can adapt.
- Nonverbal communication can set the tone for the degree of formality that you adopt with the panel.
- Details and facts about their experience can be an invitation to relate your work to their own work.

Challenge 3: Use of the Vita to Structure Inquiry

A vita can be considered a map of your competencies and a result of efforts taken to inventory your accomplishments and develop yourself as a professional on a continuous basis. The language used in this experience is one that you have spoken for many years. Professionals on your panel will be respectful of your particular conceptualization dialect, but will expect you to be fluent in the scientific discoveries and literature base that have informed our practice for the past decade. The goal is to assure the committee that you have breadth and depth in your approach to psychology. Important questions to ask as part of this process might be the following:

- What roles have I played in the field and what areas have I sought to improve?
- What are my reflective practices (include strengths and vulnerabilities in dealing with feedback)?
- How broad and specific is my experience, and how does it relate to field mastery?
- What are my most typical and atypical strategies for consumption patterns for literature in our field?
- What subjective and objective lenses do I use to examine cases?

By examining your responses to these questions you can help clarify your strengths and the biases with which you approach your work. And while clarification is an important precursor to communication about yourself to the panel, it can also serve as an impetus to delve into the vulnerabilities in knowledge or self-understanding that, once addressed, can strengthen you as a professional.

In taking self-inventory, be sure to avoid the following approaches:

- Being so task oriented that you forget to establish the same rapport that you would with clients in giving and receiving information
- Presenting a false self, an image that does not acknowledge any of your limitations
- Presenting a series of places that you've worked in lieu of roles that you've filled
- Answering questions too quickly instead of adopting the reflective stance used in your work
- Waiting to be interviewed instead of asserting your thoughts about your work

Challenge 4: Selection of Assessment Measure and Approach and Decision Making

Your approach to assessment ranges from the tools you select to the conclusions you reach. Be prepared to discuss alternatives to your approach when asked to consider other possibilities. In addressing measurement issues related to your work, consider the following questions:

- How are the measures that I use uniquely suited to address the referral question?
- Are the psychometric properties of the measures that I use satisfactory?
- How could my demeanor in the evaluation process affect the outcome of testing?
- If a diagnosis was given, what are (three) other diagnostic considerations?
- How do I keep myself abreast of updates on tests and measures in my field?

To the extent that you have accessed and used compendium guides for measures (Antony, Orsillo, & Roemer, 2001; Nezu, Ronan, Meadows, & McClure, 2000) appropriate to areas of clinical domains in which you frequently work, you will be better prepared to address the suitability of those measures used in the context of the array of measures available.

In your approach to delineating assessment, avoid the following:

- Relying too heavily on your own subjective accounts of client symptoms to validate progress
- Defending the integrity of measures for which there is little psychometric support. While it is sometimes necessary to use measures that lack this support, it is important to share the reasons for this decision (selection of the instrument, suitability for the points of evaluation)

- Reviewing details of assessment results while neglecting the big picture
- Reviewing scores on measures without linking this to how this information is helpful
- Neglect of contextual considerations in assessment

Challenge 5: Etiology From Multiple Theoretical Perspectives

In the case of Clinical Child Psychology credentialing, you will likely conceptualize your case from a theoretical perspective that you favor. In some specialties, a stronger requirement for a specific theoretical base will be present. The fundamental principles of the theory or model that you use will likely be governed by your area of expertise and the theoretical orientation to which you subscribe. A dynamic etiological presentation will appreciate the impact of multiple domains highlighted in the case conceptualization. Ask yourself the following questions:

- What central domains were used in my framework as markers for healthy functioning?
- Can I employ multiple theories to predict different components of the case?
- How can theoretical orientations account for historical as well as recent influences?
- What explanations that might not "fit" with theory might be helpful to understand the case?
- How did the theory help to explain symptoms and resolution of client needs?

In discussing causal explanations of client issues to the panel, avoid the following:

- A dogmatic approach about the explanatory power of a single theory
- Adherence to a single theory to explain problems of all clients instead of a goodness-of-fit approach
- Overlooking the importance of collaborative understanding with the client
- Failure to incorporate data from multiple parties (family) to gain multiple perspectives
- Failure to recognize role of biological or medication factors related to changes

Challenge 6: Generating Hypotheses and Case Formulation

The translation of presenting problems into goals and goals into effective treatment is predicated upon the ability to understand the causal influences of client distress, the unique aspects of a client that make him or her resilient and/or vulnerable, and the multiple pathways to symptom relief. Although not always well defined in the literature, these factors are generally referred to as case-conceptualization or case formulation skills. Case formulation relates to systemic thinking using both holistic and reductionistic techniques to understand the factors influencing the case. To accomplish this, you want to conceptualize the underlying determinants of the clients. The conceptualization will reflect the values you place on explanatory models in psychology. When asked to describe case formulation of patient(s), consider the following questions:

- What neurochemical, physiological, cognitive, affective, social, and societal domains are relevant?
- What psychological processes, internal and external, can be related to client needs?
- How can the presenting concerns of the case be viewed as adaptive and functional in the past?
- What drives motivation for a client?
- How can theories help to frame points of resolution for client needs to be met?

Be prepared to respond to the models that you have drawn upon in developing your hypotheses related to the case, using both classic studies that define early hallmark models as well as later literature that provides support for application of these models to specific problems you are addressing. To the extent that you have considered a myriad of models in your case formulation, you will be equipped to cogently set forth empirically based explanations for a wide range of panel questions. For example, a case formulation reliant on multiple models might include those that highlight motivation for change (Prochaska & Velicer, 1997); fundamental classifications of responses (Folkman, Lazarus, Dunkel-Schelter, DeLongis, & Gruen, 1986); neurobiological factors (Honk & Schutter, 2006); animal-based research support for symptom development (Willner, Muscat, & Papp, 1992); functional–analytic approaches (Nezu, Nezu, Friedman, & Haynes, 1998); contexts, including developmental, racial, ethnic, and cultural (Berg & Upchurch, 2007; Locke, 1992; Sellers et al., 1998);

and resilience factors that serve important roles in client recovery (Carver, 2002; Valentiner, Holahan, & Moos, 1994).

In conceptualizing your cases, avoid the following approaches:

- Understanding the client from only one domain that reflects a bias toward your expertise
- Overpathologizing the client's presenting symptoms
- Thinking about the client outside of his or her context (cultural, health, or disability) when context is relevant
- Focusing too much on internal (e.g., personality) or external (e.g., impoverished environment) variables
- Presentation of a clinical picture that fails to incorporate the science of psychology

Challenge 7: Treatment Technique Selection and Decision Making

In examining the techniques used to treat your case, it might be reasonable to assume that you used treatment techniques that typify those you used with other clients. In approaching the evaluation of treatment techniques used, the panel will be likely to ask two types of questions. The first relates to the selection of the technique over other available alternatives. The panel may ask you to explain the reasons for your choice of a particular treatment technique. Given the recent emphasis on empirically validated techniques, you should be familiar with references and protocols for evidence-based work in the area of your practice. The second type of question might require you to outline the decision-making process used in selection and delivery or the strategy for implementation of that technique with that particular client. To prepare for this portion of the exam, consider reviewing the following sources:

- Evidence-based practices references used to guide treatment techniques that you used
- Outcome study articles providing evidence that treatments selected are better than controls
- Meta-analysis studies that provide an overview of the outcomes of many studies
- Efficacy of alternative treatment models and techniques used to treat similar problems
- The fidelity with which you implemented the treatment technique, based on the standard

In outlining the treatment delivery to the panel, avoid the following mistakes:

- Techniques that make no use of assessment data
- Use of techniques that don't match goals
- Failure to appreciate limitations of any techniques used
- Discussions that reflect lack of knowledge of techniques whose efficacy has been contraindicated in the literature (e.g., catharsis)
- Failure to recognize alternative evidence-based techniques that might have similar efficacy

Challenge 8: Treatment Review

In the exam setting, highlighting of the case treatment must involve an appreciation for succinctness. There is simply no time to go over every element of the case. In conceptualizing your account of the work that you did, it can be useful to conceptualize your work in three different phases: beginning—what you did to build rapport and how you set goals; middle—what goals you focused on with which techniques; and end—how the maintenance of gains and how termination went from both client and therapist perspectives. In the area of treatment review, include the following strategies:

- Highlight what strengthened the alliance and discuss the challenges to the alliance.
- Affirm strategies developed by the client and therapist that contributed to specific progress.
- Identify interruptions to progress and how they were dealt with at the time.
- Identify insights gained from working with the client during the treatment implementation phase.
- Point out how change generalized from the session to life.

In highlighting your treatment approach with the client, avoid the following approaches:

- A session-by-session account of treatment. Instead, provide an overview of the techniques that were used with goals.
- An in-depth description of technique without attention to its impact
- Introduction of a technique without a clear sense of how theory explains its utility
- Advocating strongly for use of a technique with a population for which it is not typically used

- Treatments that fail to take into account the unique elements of a client's symptom(s)

Challenge 9: Practices in Consultation

Consultation experience might be addressed from two perspectives: 1) you as consultant provider and 2) you as consultant seeker. This section addresses consultation-seeking practices, which are significant because they provide assurance that biases that sometimes develop from isolation in practice can be confronted and addressed. Engagement in consultation experiences communicates an openness to new perspectives, an acknowledgement that growth is continuous, and a value system for collaborative approaches to treatment. In highlighting consultation experiences, consider presenting the following information:

- Who you selected as a mentor and what characteristics influenced your selection
- The types of situations in which you are most likely to seek consultation
- What you have gained from past consultation experiences
- The types of questions you have posed to consultants for help
- The limitations of consultation

When describing consultative experiences to the panel, avoid the following pitfalls:

- Detailing only consultation that is passive (e.g., built into the work system instead of that actively sought)
- Giving the panel too many details of a case that you brought to a consultant
- Allowing the information about a consultant to overshadow the reason you value the consultation
- Enacting the consultative process in the exam by asking panel members for their opinion
- Dealing with insecurities of trusting your own judgment in this forum

Challenge 10: Articulating Your Supervision, Teaching, and Management Style

While much of the exam relates to how you acquire information and use it to benefit the practice of psychology, the exam can also function to elucidate how you manage the process of imparting knowledge to others. To those in positions in which teaching and supervision of others is more formalized, this area is more likely to be addressed. Teaching and supervision roles include activities related to professional presentations, mentorship roles in research, and oversight of employees. In detailing characteristics of your leadership roles in the context of teaching and learning, consider

- Identifying your teaching philosophy, including a description of the motivational elements of engagement
- Being prepared to link philosophy of teaching to the philosophy of learning
- Relating markers for growth or change in students and supervisees
- Discussing your own growth experiences from teaching
- The principles of leadership that motivate your management of others

In discussing your experiences related to these leadership roles avoid

- Addressing content topics, without attending to process elements
- Exaggerating the impact of a leadership role without recognition of learner import
- Discussing how you teach or lead without recognition of or adjustment to learner style
- Neglecting attention to the developmental level of those in learner roles
- Promoting a dichotomous view of roles of leader and learner

Responding to the Written Case Vignette

During several of the board certification examinations, you will likely be asked to comment on a written vignette case introduced to you with respect to the ethics and an ethical dilemma presented in your submitted materials. Given that the latter task will likely be less demanding because you have had time to think about the ethical dilemmas prior to the exam, the portion of the exam that involves the new vignettes in the exam is addressed here. The purpose of the written vignette task, at its most basic level, is to assess your competency to recognize ethical issues at the front end of a case so that you can deal preventatively with ethical issues. According to Doverspike (1999), ethical challenges present professionals with the opportunity to think projectively and retrospectively about a case—projecting possible resolutions to dilemmas and looking back at how those actions would affect all parties involved.

To the extent that you have engaged in such processes routinely in your practice and adopted a decision-making model that is useful to you, this experience of "thinking on your feet" will be less taxing. The primary differences between the confrontation of ethical issues in your work life and the demand presented by the vignette in the exam are the time frame for responses (perhaps 15 minutes instead of 15 hours) and the inability to consult the literature or another colleague. In many cases, however, the immediacy of responding required in the vignette task parallels the demands of real-life ethical issues that come as surprises to us, with a need to immediately appreciate the risks and obligations associated with the situation. Further, the exam demand is not necessarily focused on the identification of the optimal response, but is instead to appreciate the responsibilities associated with the case. Consider framing your approach to this task by addressing the following issues:

- What ethical standards and principles are relevant in the context of the parties affected?
- What laws in my state are relevant to the case?
- What are multiple resolutions and the effects on each party in the context of stated ethical concerns?
- How might I balance my responsibility and obligations with sensitivity to the client and his or her view of my intentions?
- How might I document issues to address liability issues?

In approaching ethical issues with a panel, avoid the following practices:

- Waiting to speak until you've figured it all out. Instead, discuss the issue as you think it out.
- Neglecting discussion of a boundary crossing, even if it's immediately viewed as a violation
- Discussion of how to hold to the "letter of the law" without discussing the spirit of the standard
- Minimizing your own discussion of a dilemma by saying you would simply consult with another source about it
- Highlighting the breadth of multiple ethical issues without going in depth on any single issue (i.e., listing instead of discussing the basis for your concerns)

Telescoping in on the Trends

The regulations and conditions under which we teach and practice are all synchronous with the climate and stability of our work world. If your world has shrunk to the influences of your daily encounters, namely, those with or for whom you work or serve, allow this process to catapult you into involvement in your field. In order to protect the welfare of our clients, we need to advocate for professional responsibility. Be prepared to respond to panel questions about how your actions might be considered in the context of certain trends that affect our field. Consider the following when you address the issues facing our field and your role in representing our profession:

- What are my most deeply held convictions and areas of skepticism encountered in my practice?
- What issue-education do I receive from membership organization publications or magazines?
- What issues are raised by list serves that I subscribe to?
- What is my source of legislative updates for psychologists?
- What concerns characterize the issues that I am following (economic? client welfare)?

In communicating to the panel about current issues in our field, avoid the following:

- An approach toward advocacy that is limited to what's at stake for you
- An inability to discuss the issues that face clients served in your professional niche
- Addressing an issue solely from the perspective of how the professional is adversely affected (without addressing how the client is harmed by an issue)
- Outlining any issues without an understanding of how the profession can address it
- An outdated approach to delineating trends—is it 5 months old or 5 years old?

Summary

In all likelihood you entered the oral exam overprepared, both by your professional experiences and by your scrutiny and efforts to fill in the gaps during exam preparation. One professional reflected back on the experience by noting, "My goal—and I think this is true of others approaching ABPP—was to become a better psychologist, and for that, no preparation is too much." To the extent that you have given attention to the voice that sets forth discipline in your work, strengthened your professional self-awareness, and joined together with others in the self-evaluation process, you have completed a remarkable milestone. The acknowledgement of completing this exam process will continue to resonate with you for many years, as you maintain membership in an organization that sets standards for practice that make you proud to be part of the profession.

Linda S. Berberoglu, PhD, ABPP
Specialty in Forensic Psychology

Eric York Drogin, JD, PhD, ABPP
Specialty in Forensic Psychology

The Appeals Process

Introduction

Candidates notified by the ABPP that they have failed some aspect of the specialty certification process are likely to feel disappointed, but they should not despair. Many such candidates persevere and undertake the process again. Although official statistics are not available, our combined experiences suggest that candidates who fail some aspect of the certification process have a reasonable chance of passing the second time around, particularly when they incorporate the feedback and recommendations they received from practice sample reviewers or members of the oral examination committee.

Candidates also have the option of availing themselves of formal appeals when they receive an adverse decision at various stages of the certification process. The primary purpose of these appeals is to determine whether there were any procedural errors or violations of the specialty board's policies, and if so, whether these errors were so substantial as to have deprived the candidate of a fair examination or review.

This chapter explores the sometimes complex and time-consuming appeals process. The goal is to provide candidates with the information necessary to decide whether and how to file an appeal with a specialty board after receiving news of an adverse outcome. This chapter also includes several case vignettes that illustrate examples of successful and unsuccessful appeals.

Appealable Decisions

According to the ABPP's policies and procedures, the following decisions of the specialty board may be appealed:

1. Denial of meeting specialty-specific qualifications
2. Non-approval of practice samples and/or written examinations
3. Failure of the oral examination

This breadth of appealable decisions often comes as a surprise to candidates, who typically labor under the misperception that only oral examination failures are subject to ABPP and specialty board appellate procedures. The ABPP's Policies and Procedures provide that "an appealable decision shall not be final until the appeal process has been completed" (ABPP, 2009). What this means is that if a candidate still has a valid appeal in the works, he or she is not considered to have "failed" or to have been "denied" until that appeal has fully run its course.

Filing an Appeal

According to the ABPP's Policies and Procedures:

> The candidate may challenge an appealable decision within 30 days of receipt of written notice of that decision. The candidate must specify the grounds on which the appeal is made. The alleged grounds must be numbered and must be a violation of the Specialty Board's procedures.
>
> The appeal should be addressed to the President of the Specialty Board [SB] who in turn shall refer it to the Appeals Committee of the Specialty Board.
>
> Appeals related to the denial of meeting general requirements for candidacy shall be forwarded to the Executive Office for resolution by the ABPP Standards Committee, whose decision on these requirements is final.
>
> The decision of the SB should be affirmed unless there was a failure by the SB to adhere to its procedures. In any case, the procedural error would have to be such that it may substantially affect the decision.
>
> If the candidate demonstrates by clear and convincing evidence that there was a procedural error that harmed the candidate in a material way, the Committee shall provide a remedy. (ABPP, 2009)

As noted, determining whether and how to file an appeal can be a very complex and time-consuming process. Do you want to expend the additional time and effort necessary to pursue an appeal, effectively throwing good time—and thus the money that your time represents—after bad? Is the specialty board going to be insulted by you filing an appeal, and interpret your doing so as defensive, thus reducing in some fashion your odds of prevailing in a subsequent examination? Is the potentially drawn-out appeals process going to delay still further your eventual obtainment of this credential? These are all legitimate and substantial questions that should be approached with due consideration of the individual candidate's patience, resources, planned career arc, and access to appropriate peer consultation.

Timing becomes an issue from the outset of a potential appeal, and should be supported by the same careful documentation that the candidate would apply to the receipt and issuance of any other professional correspondence. When was the "written notice" of the specialty board's decision actually "received"? Candidates who were away on vacation, ill, or otherwise unable to obtain the letter in question may wish to request an extension. Does the specialty board use any different schedule for processing appeals, regardless of whether this is actually consistent with the ABPP's policies and procedures? Candidates should scan the letters they receive with this in mind, and may wish to revisit the specialty board's own Web site to make sure of the relevant timelines; for example, some specialty boards specify one deadline for notification that an appeal is pending, and another for actually filing the appeal itself.

With one eye on the calendar, candidates should consider how comfortably they then can build a "cooling-off" period into their decision-making and correspondence strategies. Penning and mailing the classic same-day "Dear Ignoramuses" reply letter is no more effective in dealing with specialty boards than it is in response to inquiries from one's state licensing board. Similarly, initiating telephone or e-mail contact with the ABPP, with various specialty board members, or—in particular—with one's examiners is a definitely counterproductive undertaking. Candidates should confine their arguments to the appeal itself, addressed to the president of the specialty board in accordance with ABPP's policies and procedures.

In order to meet an appellate standard that is highly specific in some aspects and somewhat vague in others, candidates will need to obtain and organize some additional information as soon as possible. The requirement to "specify" and "number" the grounds for an appeal that constitute a "violation of the specialty board's procedures" calls upon candidates to determine just what those procedures are. These may or may not be included in written materials received prior to the examination, or posted on the specialty board Web site. What, for example, are the specific rules that examiners are supposed to follow? If these aren't readily accessible, candidates may wish to request them from the specialty board, and request an extended deadline for filing the appeal if receipt of such materials is significantly delayed.

What are the data on which the examiners or practice sample reviewers based their individual and group decisions? Did they fill out and exchange forms, or engage in face-to-face, telephonic, fax-based, or e-mail discussion? Where are these data? How quickly can they be obtained? Was the oral examination itself audio- or videotaped? Is the protocol of the written examination preserved, along with methods and results of computerized or hand scoring? What is the psychometrically sound methodology by which the oral and written examinations were constructed, and by whom? How, for example, were specific content areas selected and apportioned in terms of their relative weight in overall scoring? Has the specialty board or its designee conducted any follow-up validation of these assessments? What were the results? Candidates are being asked to establish by "clear and convincing evidence" the presence of a "procedural error" that harmed them in a "material way." This substantial evidentiary burden should be addressed with an appropriate array of objective information.

Appeals should never be undertaken merely as a "fishing expedition," and in our experience as specialty board members, successful appeals tend to focus on those aspects truly likely to have occasioned "material" harm to one's candidacy, in contrast to a scattershot approach listing everything that *might* have gone wrong with the examination in question.

Scope and Conduct of the Appeal

According to ABPP's policies and procedures:

> The Appeals Committee reviewing the appeal must complete its review within 60 days after receipt of the request for appeal letter. . ..
>
> The procedural issues addressed by the Appeals Committee shall be limited to those stated in the appeal request letter and which meet the requirement of an appealable procedural issue.
>
> If legal issues appear to be involved the Appeals Committee may consult with the ABPP legal counsel.
>
> The Appeals Committee shall implement a process of review primarily based upon information before the SB at the time of the decision. The Appeals Committee may seek further information from the Chair and members of the Oral Examination, the Credentials Review Committee, the Practice Sample reviewers, the candidate, or others as appropriate to the issues raised. The process is not a de novo review, but a review of the challenge to the SB decision.
>
> The Appeals Committee shall confer as soon as possible upon the SB's receipt of the candidate's letter requesting an appeal and shall complete its review and decision, addressing each issue(s) raised by the appellant, within

60 days. Failure to complete the review in the 60-day period shall move the appeal to the Board of Trustees for resolution. . . .

The report of the Appeals Committee shall address each issue raised by the candidate and its decision related thereto and the basis for that decision. The report shall be forwarded to the Executive Officer [EO] through the SB President. The report shall then be forwarded to the candidate under the EO's signature on the ABPP stationary [sic]. Editing for format and for legal considerations on advice of the ABPP legal counsel may be undertaken by the EO if necessary. (ABPP, 2009)

Given the importance of deadlines to this construct, candidates should make sure that the appeal letter is sent with "return receipt requested." If the 60-day period lapses without the appeals committee having completed its review, the appeal automatically moves to the ABPP Board of Trustees.

Is there a practical difference between 1) simply "appealing the appeal" even after the 60-day period has lapsed, and 2) having the appeal moved directly to the Board of Trustees? Arguably so, for if the specialty board's review is particularly negative, the candidate may wish to assert that in its incomplete form it should not be taken into consideration—in other words, specifically "not read"—by the ABPP, and that failure to take this approach could constitute a violation of ABPP's own policies and procedures. This would depend, of course, on whether the specialty board's review ever made it as far as "the Executive Officer through the SB President" for signature and potential vetting by ABPP's legal counsel.

On the other hand, the candidate who feels that the specialty board has botched his or her examination, and who further concludes that the appeals committee's response stands as yet further evidence that the specialty board just doesn't "get it," may be glad not only to put the alleged flawed board work on display, but also take advantage of a "second bite at the apple" that specifically refutes the appeals committee's arguments. For example, the appeals committee may have failed to "address each issue raised by the candidate and its decision related thereto and the basis for that decision"—in all, three distinct but interrelated components.

Candidates who do decide to mount a separate ABPP Board of Trustees "appeal of the appeal" should bear in mind that the subject matter of this second appeal is limited to issues raised in the initial appeal. However, this shouldn't prevent the candidate from being specific about what he or she considers inadequate aspects of the specialty board's review of that initial appeal. Does the specialty board provide its own instructions to appeals committee members—instructions that those members failed to follow, or that run contrary to the ABPP's Policies and Procedures, or that were never authorized by the ABPP?

Appeals Committee Structure

According to the ABPP's Policies and Procedures:

> In the past the ABPP had a single, national appeal committee. Each Specialty Board (SB) now must establish an Appeals Committee. This change is consistent with the organization's current structure and more specific to each specialty's perspective. . . .
>
> SBs may adopt supplementary rules and procedures, which are consistent with these policies, and submit them to the BOT/Executive Committee so they will be available for CO Staff's information. . . .
>
> The SB shall establish a standing Appeals Committee of 3 members appointed from its Board Members, who ordinarily are not involved in the examination. If one or more members of the Appeals Committee are unable or not eligible to serve, the SB shall appoint the necessary alternates or members of the Appeals Committee.

Candidates requesting that a specialty board reconsider the denial of an appeal—or who decide instead to "appeal the appeal" directly to ABPP—may wish to inquire into the following issues:

1. Is the appeals committee truly a "standing" one, or was it instead an ad hoc affair, put together by the specialty board for a particular round of examinations, or for this particular appeal? Presumably, the rationale for a standing committee includes not only convenience of assignment but also the opportunity to develop individual and corporate expertise in addressing complex issues in accordance with established policies. What was the motivation for any ad hoc composition, and did this arguably work to the disadvantage of the candidate?

2. Does the appeals committee truly consist of three members, or is it instead either understaffed or overstaffed? In particular, the participation of less than three members would mean that only one or two persons made a decision typically assigned to a group. If the specialty board found it necessary to add one or more additional members, what was the reason? Does this reflect a lack of relevant expertise on the part of the usual members? If so, was the negative opinion of an additional member given undue weight, or was the positive opinion of a truly qualified additional member seemingly overlooked?

3. Is the appeals committee truly comprised of specialty board members? Again, relevant and long-standing expertise in specialty board procedures

is presumably the reason for this requirement. There is more to judging the ABPP-specific sufficiency of credentials, clinical functioning, and examination performance than current practice in the field and one's own ability to have met arguably similar standards many years ago. Along these lines, do any non-specialty board members of the appeals committee in fact *still* practice in the field, and were they provided with documentation on updated appeals procedures prior to rendering a decision in this matter?

4. Were members of the appeals committee involved in the overall examination process? Presumably the primary reason for discouraging this practice is that conflicts of interest are likely to arise. Candidates will certainly have reason to question the objectivity of an appeals committee member who has already rendered a negative decision concerning the case at hand. More generally, is an appeals committee member currently involved in the specialty board's examination process going to be regarded as overinvested in the way examinations are being conducted? The specialty board is unlikely to want to cultivate the potential appearance of impropriety in this fashion.

5. Were any supplanted members of the appeals committee truly either "unable" or "not eligible" to serve? What was the basis for this determination, and by whom was it made? Did the member in question have a legitimate conflict of interest, an acute incapacitation, or supervening scheduling conflict that would have pushed consideration of the appeal beyond acceptable temporal limits, or, for example, did the specialty board's office assistant get shunted to voice mail on the first telephone call and decide at that point to hang up and go to the next name on the list? Along these lines, was the ultimate decision to appoint an "alternate" or "member" truly made by the specialty board in accordance with its corporate bylaws, and did any appointment to "alternate" instead of "member" carry with it any disparity in participation, including time to review as well as time to participate in any group discussion?

6. Finally, were any "supplementary rules and procedures" adopted by the specialty board, in accordance with its corporate bylaws, instead of being adopted by the appeals committee on its own? Were such "rules and procedures" truly "supplementary" and not "alternative," and therefore "consistent" with the ABPP's Policies and Procedures? Were such rules and procedures actually submitted to the ABPP's Board of Trustees or its executive committee? If so, how were they received by the ABPP, and were they properly in place by the time the appeals committee commenced its deliberations on the case in question?

Remedies

According to the ABPP's Policies and Procedures:

> The remedy will ordinarily be to void an oral examination (or practice sample review) and offer a new examination (or practice sample review) with no additional fees assessed to the candidate, or to refer the matter back to the examination committee. In extraordinary circumstances, another remedy may be provided. The Appeals Committee, however, may not "pass" a candidate or regrade an examination.

In other words, neither the ABPP nor the specialty board's appeals committee can grant board certification as a sole result of appellate proceedings; however, note that one remedy may be to "refer the matter back to the examination committee." This, in fact, may prompt a reconsideration that results in a "pass" after all. The potential ramifications of this option are so substantial that candidates may want in their appeal letters to emphasize, if appropriately supported by the circumstances, that the appeals committee's specific errors may warrant resolution by such reconsideration.

It is unclear what might constitute "another remedy" in the context, above and beyond such potentially overlapping options as voiding the initial procedure, offering a free new procedure, and directing the initial examiners to try again. Perhaps under whatever constitute "extraordinary circumstances" the new procedure could be limited to readdressing just one aspect of the initial one, or fees for the initial, botched procedure might actually be refunded, or re-examination could be conducted with reference to an expedited timetable. Candidates will take comfort at the notion that "extraordinary circumstances" do not appear necessary for the appeals committee to "refer the matter back to the examination committee."

Vignettes

The following vignettes may help to illustrate some of the issues described in this chapter.

"Non-Starter" Appeal: The Case of Dr. Public

Upon notification that he had failed his written examination, John Q. Public, PhD, wrote a letter to the ABPP office manager stating that the examination was "unsound" and asserting that his candidacy should be judged instead on the basis of "my documented experience and my future performance on practice samples and the oral examination." Informed that his appeal should be directed to the specialty board president, Dr. Public submitted a letter approx-imately 3 months later, claiming without further elaboration that "the written examination is unfair, unscientific, and biased," and requesting an opportu-nity to "address the same topic areas in an oral examination format" in order to demonstrate "my mastery of the field in which I have practiced successfully for so many years." Dr. Public's appeal letter did not number the allegations or tie them to any identifiable specialty board procedures.

The specialty board president informed Dr. Public via return mail that while this appeal was barred due to formatting issues and the passage of time, the specialty board allowed candidates to take the written examination a total of three times. Dr. Public was also asked to provide the specialty board, at his convenience, with further information about the difficulties he had experi-enced, so the written examination committee could review these concerns "in order to ensure that our procedures are conducted with appropriate con-cern for scientific rigor and fundamental fairness."

An Unsuccessful Appeal: The Case of Dr. Doe

Upon notification that she had failed her oral examination, Jane K. Doe, EdD, wrote to the specialty board president that her examiners had commit-ted several errors, which she tied to specific aspects of the specialty board's online summary of "Oral Examination Rules and Procedures." Specifically, she alleged that "Dr. Hernandez made repeated reference to my having utilized 'WAIS-III' when my practice samples indicated that I utilized the 'WAIS-IV' throughout"; that "Dr. Kline asked me to describe what sorts of informed consent procedures I typically used with my clients, despite the fact that both practice samples reflected court-ordered interventions for which no informed consent was required"; and that "the overall demeanor of the examiners was lacking in both warmth and friendliness, such that I got the impression they were less interested in me as a person than in whether I met some abstract, technical 'standard' for clinical practice."

The specialty board president responded via return mail that the appeals com-mittee had reviewed Dr. Doe's appeal, and had found that (1) reference to the WAIS-III instead of the WAIS-IV was inaccurate but ultimately not harmful, particularly since Dr. Doe's explanation of her use of the WAIS-IV met with the approval of all three examiners; (2) informed consent was such a central component of psychological service delivery that it was reasonable to inquire into Dr. Doe's approach to this, especially since she had indicated that only 20% of her work involved "court-ordered interventions" that allegedly did not require informed consent; and (3) while the validity of Dr. Doe's regrettable subjective experience was not being questioned, all three examiners had conducted themselves with an appropriate degree of collegiality and professionalism. The specialty board president further noted that Dr. Doe's negative outcome had been a "close call," that all three oral examiners had praised her ethical sensitivity and her "clear potential for enhanced skill with additional supervision," and that it was the specialty board's hope that Dr. Doe—and other candidates like her—remain in the certification process.

A Successful Appeal: The Case of Dr. Chang

Upon notification that she had failed her oral examination, Christine Chang, PsyD, wrote to the specialty board president that her examiners had committed several errors, which she tied to specific aspects of the specialty board's "Oral Examination Rules and Procedures," as distributed to examiners upon their agreement to participate. Dr. Chang had specifically requested this document from the specialty board president, along with copies of the "Examinee Rating Forms" filled out by each examiner at the conclusion of the examination.

Dr. Chang's numbered and cross-referenced allegations included the following: (1) that "Dr. Jones was repeatedly and pointedly critical of my having reported the client's dangerous behavior, despite the existence of a state law—a copy of which is attached—that required me to do so"; (2) that "all three examiners based their negative conclusions substantially on my 'lack of familiarity with legal requirements' as reflected on Form B2"; and (3) that "the chair of my panel incorrectly summed the individual examiners' numerical ratings, and thus failed to conclude that another round of voting was called for by your specialty board's enumerated rules and procedures."

The specialty board president responded via return mail that the appeals committee had reviewed Dr. Chang's appeal, had found that all three of her allegations were substantiated, and had concluded that "each of these procedural errors clearly harmed Dr. Chang's candidacy in a material way." The proposed solution—with apologies—was (1) that the initial oral examination be voided; (2) that Dr. Chang be afforded another oral examination, free of charge, on the same practice samples; and (3) that this examination be scheduled during the week of Dr. Chang's choosing within the next 60 days.

Summary

One of the primary objectives of this chapter was to demystify the ABPP appeals process. We have intentionally highlighted the complexities involved in the proper preparation and filing of an appeal so that candidates contemplating such action are aware at the outset of the potential time demands they may face. Feelings of frustration and disappointment are understandable reactions to failing some aspect of the certification process, but in and of themselves, such feelings are an insufficient basis for a successful appeal. We realize that many candidates who fail some phase of the certification process will forego an appeal and simply opt to undertake the certification process again. For those candidates contemplating a challenge to an adverse decision, we hope this chapter contains ample explanation, appropriately cautionary statements, and plenty of practical advice.

W. Michael Nelson, III, PhD, ABPP
Specialties in Clinical and Clinical
Child and Adolescent Psychology

Kathleen J. Hart, PhD, ABPP
Specialty in Clinical Child and
Adolescent Psychology

Giving Back to the ABPP

Introduction

So what do you do after your ABPP examination? First, congratulate yourself! You have joined the ranks of a small but growing number of board-certified individuals in our profession. Currently, there are approximately 3,200 ABPP-certified professionals in the United States, and the number is growing. There are about 120 new certifications awarded annually. As you know, going through the self-awareness and reflection process necessary to become board certified is a rigorous one in which your competencies in your specialty area are carefully assessed. After the ABPP certification process, individuals often pause and acknowledge their hard work and feel pride in what they have accomplished. After completing the ABPP board certification process, it is likely that you have pondered the question: So what can I do now to further support the understanding, value, and accessibility of ABPP board certification?

To a large extent, the answer to this question depends on the point in your career at which you have achieved diplomate status. For those candidates who achieved the diplomate within the first 10–15 years of their professional lives, their contributions to the profession will likely have a different focus than that of those who attain this status at a later point, when the diplomate will serve as a "crowning moment" in an already distinguished career. As such, your personal and professional stage of life will influence your answers to the question, "What do I do after I pass my ABPP examination?"

To answer the question of where you go next, it is helpful to briefly reflect on where you have been. All who have attained ABPP status are alike in many ways, have jumped through a number of the same hoops, and have reached the post-ABPP point in their careers. Figure 12.1 provides a schematic representation of the common hurdles overcome in the journey to becoming an ABPP board-certified psychologist.

Figure 12.1 depicts the typical regulatory and evaluative sequence that we psychologists have encountered, from the day we first enrolled in a doctoral program to the point when we achieved the highest credential of specialty board certification that is most clearly recognized in the United States. In our development as psychologists, we have been evaluated throughout our entire careers. Starting with being accepted into a psychology program, we are indirectly evaluated through reviews of our doctoral programs (e.g., APA accreditation) and directly evaluated through individual reviews (e.g., doctoral qualifying exams, dissertation defenses, state licensure exams, board certification by the ABPP). Once we have graduated from an accredited program

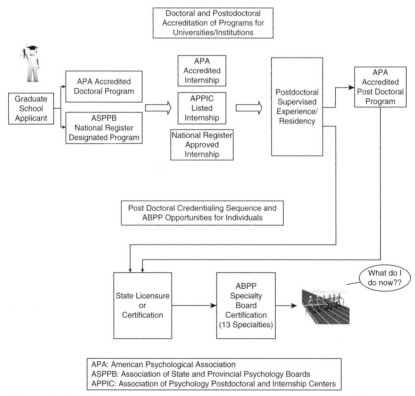

Figure 12.1 The Route to ABPP Board Certification. APA, American Psychological Association; APPIC, Association of Psychology Postdoctoral and Internship Centers; ASPPB, Association of State and Provincial Psychology Boards.

in psychology, the regulatory and evaluative task shifts from determining if programs meet established training standards to asking if we, as individual psychologists, meet the educational and competency standards to be certified not only for generic independent practice (i.e., through state licensure) but also for specialized practice (i.e., through specialized ABPP status). Although there are ways in which the six regulatory functions differ, they all serve the same fundamental purpose—quality assurance for consumer protection. This is particularly important in this day and age when the provision of mental health services has become increasingly complex and competitive.

As an ABPP diplomate, you have reached a pinnacle by demonstrating that you have the proper educational background, supervised experienced, and competencies to be board certified as a specialist in 1 of 13 ABPP specialties (see Table 1.1 in Chapter 1). The way in which health and mental health services are delivered in our society has changed dramatically, and likely will continue to change. Factors such as the current climate in which mental health practitioners work, managed care, mandated continued education requirements, and the increased importance of specialization all likely influenced your decision to obtain a credential documenting that you have reached the highest level of professional competency in your specialty area. However, for many of us, it is likely that these factors are really secondary to our desire to strive for excellence and our drive to measure ourselves against the highest standards recognized in our profession, namely that of ABPP board certification.

For many of you, however, arriving at the post-ABPP point is a "breath of fresh air," with the fleeting thought that you have "run the gauntlet and are now finished!" After a post-reinforcement lag, it is likely that many of you will reflect on how you can show appreciation to the profession that has given you so much in terms of a career and identity as a psychologist.

Webster's Dictionary defines "appreciation" as "grateful recognition, as of benefit." Typically, appreciation inspires a desire to express that appreciation in an obvious way, or to "repay" what has been given. So, how can you give back to the profession that has been your chosen career and life's work? In contemplating this question, there are a variety of avenues that the newly board-certified psychologist can pursue. You now have the opportunity to participate in the advancement of the special practice of psychology at the local, state, and national levels through the governance of the ABPP and the specialty academies. This can be done in a number of ways: 1) proudly display your ABPP credentials, and advocate for a broader recognition of those credentials; 2) be a role model for your colleagues; 3) serve as a mentor for those at varying stages of contemplating or actively seeking board certification; and 4) become involved in the specialty board or academy. Each of these areas is discussed in greater detail below.

Displaying ABPP Credentials and Advocating for Their Acceptance

Display of your ABPP credentials can serve as a way to inform, educate, and encourage others to seek board certification. Although you have probably already done this, you should identify yourself as a board-certified specialist on your letterhead, professional business cards, Web sites, or any other venue where you include your degree status. Designation of board certification can follow any of the following formats:

1. John Doe, (degree), ABPP
2. Kathleen Doe, (degree), ABPP-Specialty or ABPP (Specialty)
3. Harry Doe, (degree), Board Certified in (Specialty) Psychology, ABPP
4. Sally Doe, (degree), Board Certified in (Specialty) Psychology, American Board of Professional Psychology
5. Michael Doe, (degree), Diplomate in (Specialty) Psychology, ABPP
6. Jane Doe, (degree), Diplomate in (Specialty) Psychology, American Board of Professional Psychology
7. Joseph Doe, (degree), ABPP, Board Certified (Specialty)

Psychologists in more than one specialty may use the following options:

a. Jane Doe (degree), ABPP certified (or Diplomate) in (Specialty) and certified (or Diplomate) in (Specialty)
b. The "ABPP", above, may be placed following the last specialty designation.

To accommodate a situation in which multiple psychologists are listed and all of them have ABPP certification in the same specialty, a heading such as "Board-Certified Specialists qualified by the American Board of Professional Psychology" may be used.

The ABPP is widely known and highly regarded among psychologists, and the concept of being board certified is recognized by many outside the profession; this is very highly regarded in the medical specialties. Generally, the public is now more knowledgeable about the significance of being board certified. What is not as well understood outside the profession and especially by the public is that there are many "vanity" boards that give the title of "board certified," but do so based on varying degrees of rigor in evaluating credentials and competencies. For some "vanity" boards, credentialing may include little more than completing a basic application and paying a fee. It is incumbent upon us to better inform the public and even agencies within which we work that not all "board-certified" psychologists are the same. As an ABPP board-certified psychologist, it is important to carefully investigate the merits of certification procedures of other boards so that you can knowledgably inform others about the differences between ABPP board certification and that of other boards. You can use this information to help colleagues make informed decisions about the type of board certification they want to pursue and better familiarize them with the ABPP "brand."

As discussed in detail in the beginning chapters of this book, there are some tangible benefits to being board certified by ABPP. For example, some professional liability insurance carriers offer discounts to individuals who are board certified by the ABPP (e.g., American Professional Agency, Inc). If your insurance company does not offer a discount, you might consider educating the company about the ABPP and requesting a discount. Similarly, some organizations such as the Veteran's Administration and the military branches offer step increases in pay for those who are board certified. If your hospital, organization, or agency does not offer that incentive, you could request one. Particularly if you are employed in a medical facility, making the case that such incentives be offered to physicians who are board certified would likely be helpful.

It should also be noted that many states and providences in Canada recognize the ABPP board certification as a partial waiver for licensure in other states or providences, for applicants who already maintain a license to practice psychology in another state or province. This was the primary reason that the Certificate of Professional Qualification (CPQ) was developed—to facilitate licensure reciprocity and mobility. As discussed in Chapter 2, holding an ABPP diplomate is one of the main threshold requirements in qualifying an individual for the CPQ, so the ABPP allows psychologists to become licensed more easily in other jurisdictions where they might want to practice.

Keep in mind that board certification in psychological specialties is the best means of confirming expertise in a particular area. As such, it is likely that board certification, as in medicine and surgery, will likely become the norm in the future credentialing of all psychologists. As Bent, Packard, and Goldberg (1999) wrote, "It is not the exceptional specialist who should be board certified, but the specialist who is not board certified [who] should be the exception" (p. 14). Thus, it is incumbent upon us to keep this message in the forefront of our professional activities to not only protect the future of our profession but also define advanced qualifications and standards of excellence in the field of psychology as it continues to grow. Taking such an active stance does not imply that professional psychologists who do not obtain board certification are less professional. What it does mean is that there are many competent psychologists within the field who have not been through the ABPP board certification process. As a profession, we must responsibly ask ourselves whether we have obtained the credentials that best reflect our true expertise within the field.

Being a Role Model

Being a role model to other professionals in your community can involve simply having gone through the board certification process, which currently only about 5% of U.S. psychologists have done. As a role model, you can now hold yourself up to the community as having met the highest standard of a responsible professional offering specialty services to the public. For example, your ABPP certification might be highlighted in the yellow pages and other ways of publicizing your services to the community. The fact that you are now board certified means that you have, at least in some way, wrestled with the question of why someone should seek board certification and jump through another hoop after spending a minimum of 9 years to obtain a bachelor's, master's, and a doctoral degree, to say nothing of the required supervision for licensure most states require to obtain a generic license to practice psychology. You have realized the responsibility of the individual psychologist to obtain the board certification credentials that reflect specialty training and qualify you as being competent in your stated field.

We have certainly reached a point where specialty board certification has become an essential step in assuring both clients and other professionals that one has met the qualifications to practice in a particular area of specialization. Furthermore, as the field of psychology becomes more specialized, specialty board certification is more likely to be among the requirements in specialty areas such as neuropsychology, clinical, forensic, and health psychology (Dattilio, 2002). In fact, this was the original reason that the National Register of Health Service Providers in Psychology was formed; third-party payers could readily identify clinical psychologists in the field. Now, with increasing specialization, it is important that third-party payers, as well as the public and other professions, have a means by which to identify competent psychology specialists.

As a board-certified psychologist, you are in a unique position to educate not only colleagues and clients but also administrators in the workplace (e.g., universities, hospitals, mental health agencies, managed-care companies, the military) about the importance of having board-certified psychologists on their faculty and staff, as another way such agencies and organizations can document and market themselves to the public. By employing professionals who have reached the highest standards of training and performance in their specific field, the organization can advertise its services as reaching the highest standards as well.

For example, psychologists in certain government agencies (e.g., federal prison system, VA hospitals, U.S. Public Health Service, U.S. Department of Defense) can earn higher pay for being board certified. At a number of universities, particularly those whose training follows a practitioner–scientist or scientist–practitioner model, faculty can be encouraged to obtain their ABPP certification by counting this as a refereed article or even as a prerequisite to move into the role of professor. It can be argued that attaining ABPP certification is comparable to having an article published in a refereed journal, as both involve peer review of one's work. More specifically, the ABPP process is a standard, rigorous evaluation of one's clinical professional competencies by a group of board-certified peers, in the same way that a manuscript is reviewed by experts in the author's field. By having board-certified faculty engaging in training and supervision, the institution can ensure and document that its faculty are of the highest caliber.

Responsibilities of Being a Role Model

With the credential of ABPP comes the responsibility of maintaining oneself in a manner that befits the specialty. At a minimum, this means remaining current with the field in general as well as with the specialty. One must also conduct one's professional life with the highest ethical standards, and encourage others to lead their professional lives using current standards of care and ethical conduct.

Mentoring

Mentoring your colleagues through the ABPP process is an important way to advance the profession and "give back" to the ABPP (mentoring is addressed more completely in Chapter 8; we will address some core issues here). Mentoring can be done in both informal and formal ways. Informal mentoring would likely start with helping colleagues begin to answer the question,

"Why seek ABPP board certification at all?" for themselves. See Chapter 2 for more information on how to motivate the people you mentor.

It may be helpful to conceptualize the mentoring of colleagues from a developmental framework. The stages-of-change model originally described by Prochaska, DiClemente and Norcross (1998) outlines how, in therapy, people progress through several predictable, well-defined stages in their quest to change. This type of model also can be applied to the board certification process (Chapman, 2005; Nelson & Finch, 2005). In fact, you may notice that the various stages discussed later in the chapter follow the chapters and advice contained in this book.

The first task is to assess the current "stage" of the individual whom you want to encourage to apply for ABPP certification. Many individuals may be in the *precontemplation* phase—they are not at all ready to take action and basically have no real intention of changing their behavior. These individuals may not see the usefulness or necessity of board certification or specialization because of a lack of information or ignorance about the changing face of health-care delivery in the United States today. They may ask, "What good is board certification?" or "Why do I even need it?" Remember, precontemplators typically are not prepared to take in much information directly and are best helped by observations about the benefits of board certification for themselves and for the profession.

Individuals in the *contemplation* phase are aware of the benefits of board certification and can describe how board certification demonstrates an advanced level of competence in a particular area. These individuals recognize that the field of psychology has experienced exponential growth, to the point where everything cannot be mastered. It may also be important at this stage to raise the issue of "vanity" boards, which claim to identify practitioners qualified in specialty areas, typically in a superficial manner. Here, educating colleagues about the real differences between the ABPP process and other board-certifying bodies can be helpful. Contemplators seriously consider taking action but are not ready to do so in the immediate future. In other words, they have not yet made a commitment to take action, likely because they still feel daunted by the effort required for the ABPP examination process. Your gentle encouragement of these individuals to pursue the ABPP process, along with your expression of confidence that they possess the necessary skills to succeed, will be very helpful.

In the *preparation* stage, individuals actually have a plan of action and are intending to take action in the immediate future. These individuals may have already gone to the ABPP Web site or downloaded the application materials. They may have "mapped out" in their mind an action plan and may have even "gone public" with their desire to do so by informing others. Still, there are twinges of ambivalence about actually moving forward in the process. Emphasizing the collegial format of the exams will be helpful at this stage, along with encouragement that they can be successful. Humor can also be helpful at this stage (e.g., "If I can do this, surely you can too!").

In the *action* stage, individuals have taken concrete steps in the process of obtaining board certification. The initial paperwork is likely to be completed and they may have gone through the initial phase of board certification, the credential review. At this point, the mentor can assist individuals by providing support and direction, and dealing with any irrational self-defeating beliefs that the process is too difficult to accomplish or that the goal is too high to attain. Those in the action stage might respond best to specific, direct action information about the concrete steps involved in the process.

With the stages-of-change model in mind, you can encourage and mentor an individual through the developmental passage into board certification in professional psychology. You should realize that not all potential candidates are at the action stage, or even want to be. Go slowly and assess your colleague's stage of change. You might ask at any point if he or she is concerned about any particular issue being a problem in moving toward board certification.

Having survived the process of ABPP certification, you are intimately familiar with the three (or four) stages required, and you can serve as an informational resource to individuals who are considering or have begun to pursue ABPP certification. To refresh your memory, stage I involves the application and credentials review. During this stage, the applicant submits an application form, fee, transcripts, and educational and professional credentials to the ABPP central office. The central office establishes the appropriateness of the degree in psychology and internship, confirms state licensure, and inquires about any ethical violations. Following generic approval by the central office, the material is forwarded to the specialty board, which reviews the materials to see if they meet requirements for the specialty. If the credentials are accepted, the candidate enters stage II, which varies somewhat according to specialty. Two boards (Clinical Neuropsychology and Forensic Psychology) require a written exam of specialty knowledge; at this point in time, the other boards do not.

Candidates who pass the written exam in these areas move on to the stage III; for the other specialty areas not requiring a written exam, this is stage II.

In this stage, the candidate prepares practice samples that are reviewed by a designated specialty coordinator initially, then submitted to an examining committee for review. As would be expected, the nature of the practice sample varies somewhat by specialty. In all cases, the practice sample should reflect what the candidate typically does in his or her professional practice, rather than being exemplary situations. There are minor variations in how practice samples are evaluated, but once the candidate's practice sample is accepted by the examination committee, the candidate progresses to stage III (stage IV in Clinical Neuropsychology and Forensic Psychology), which is the oral examination. The oral exam takes anywhere from 3 to 6 hours, depending on the specialty, and is often viewed by candidates as being a very stimulating and rewarding experience.

Throughout these stages, the ABPP candidate will find the process less intimidating if he or she has a "shoulder to lean on" or at least someone who can answer questions or provide encouragement. These are activities that an "informal" mentor can provide. Throughout the process it is important to note that board certification or specialty-level standing is conceptualized as higher than the basic level of requisite knowledge and skills certified by jurisdictional licensure, but well within the reach of most competent practitioners of professional psychology.

Formal mentoring is also available to most candidates in the ABPP process. Such mentoring is provided through the specialty academies (described in greater detail later in the chapter), and the specialties vary considerably in how they conduct the mentoring. For example, Clinical Neuropsychology supports a Web site called BRAIN (Be Ready for the ABPP in Neuropsychology), which emerged from a group of aspiring diplomates and grew into a support network that the Academy of Neuropsychology adopted (see Chapter 6 for more information). The BRAIN Web site offers a wide variety of resources to assist in preparation for the written exam and practice samples. No other academy offers anything quite this elaborate, but many academies, including Forensic Psychology and Clinical Psychology, offer continuing education workshops that provide detailed information about the ABPP process.

Academies also serve as the point of contact between ABPP candidates who would like a mentor and academy members (who, by definition, have attained ABPP status) who are willing to serve in that capacity. ABPP candidates who wish to find a mentor should contact the ABPP central office or the academy president, to be matched to a mentor. (Contact information for the ABPP central office and the academies can be found through the ABPP Web site at: http://abpp.org; this site offers contact information for other resources related to the ABPP process and the specialty boards.) Some academies provide specific training for those individuals interested in being mentors, whereas others use a less formal process. For information about the process in your academy, or to offer your services as a mentor, contact your academy president through the ABPP Web site.

Regardless of whether you are considering mentoring on a formal or informal basis, it is important to consider the limits of what a mentor can offer to an ABPP candidate. Keep in mind that the aim of the ABPP process is to evaluate the *applicant's* skills and abilities. As a result, it is important to ensure that the work products and other materials submitted for evaluation reflect the candidate's work and ability. Certainly, recommending that a candidate rewrite a document to increase its clarity or consider how he or she might want to express his or her ideas is within appropriate limits. Trying to recall questions from the written exam as a way of coaching an applicant, rewriting an applicant's report or personal statement, or providing crib notes to respond to anticipated questions in the oral exam are beyond the limits of mentoring.

Finally, it is important to view the mentoring process as just that—a *process* through which you will assist the applicant, using different skills, knowledge, and strategies to meet his or her particular needs at any given point in time. From your patience and motivation to initiate the board certification application, to your expressions of encouragement, you can provide important support for, and become actively involved in, the ABPP process of others. Keep your specialty board and academy informed of your efforts, as they may provide additional support, such as letters of encouragement, in this important recruitment endeavor. Mentoring also attests to your continued interest in the ABPP and may even serve as a springboard to become further involved in board or academy activities, if you so desire.

Involvement in a Specialty Board or Academy

The ABPP organization is governed by the Board of Trustees (BOT), which oversees the work of the 13 specialty boards and the central office. The central office maintains the central directory of specialists and oversees the generic candidacy verification process, among other duties. The central office also collects fees for each examination stage and annual dues. Each specialty board (e.g., Clinical Psychology, School Psychology, Rehabilitation Psychology) is responsible for developing and conducting the ABPP specialty examinations; each board has established its own examination guidelines and parameters.

Most specialty boards also have a "sister" academy that offers services such as mentoring to ABPP candidates, continuing education, candidate recruitment, advocacy of the specialty, and other duties that do not fall under the purview of the specialty board. In many cases, boards and academies work collaboratively to promote the specialty.

Attaining the ABPP diplomate qualifies you for membership in the academy of that specialty. The academies also provide opportunities for professional fellowship, advocacy activities, and recruitment. They can constitute a forum in which to work toward improving quality and accessibility of services and address other issues unique to the specialty. Both the specialty boards and the academies are volunteer organizations and thus are generally open to, and appreciative of, the help of its members.

Specialty Boards

As previously stated, the specialty board oversees the specialty examinations for its area. The size of specialty boards varies, generally by the size of the specialty; large specialty boards, such as Clinical Psycholgy, make use of regional representatives who assist in coordinating the examinations of candidates. Many specialty boards rely on members of their specialty to assist in conducting examinations, and readily accept offers of assistance from board-certified members to serve on examination committees. Although some specialty boards (e.g., Psychoanalysis) require that one has participated in training sessions prior to serving on examination committees, others (e.g., Cognitive and Behavioral Psychology, Clinical Psychology, and Clinical Child and Adolescent Psychology) use an apprentice model for examiners. In this model, a novice examiner serves as an examination committee member along with more experienced examiners at least three times before serving as an examination committee chair. Service as an ABPP examiner in your specialty area ensures that others meet the same standards and competencies required by your specialty. Many examiners also find that they learn a great deal about specific areas within the specialty when they serve in that role.

Some specialty boards (e.g., Clinical Psychology and Clinical Neuropsychology) maintain active listservs that help inform their members about activities and organizational needs. Through the listserv, one can learn how the organization operates and can volunteer when board positions become vacant, or offer to serve as an examiner. If your specialty board does not have an active listserv, contact the specialty-board president or regional representative so you can express your interest in becoming involved (contact information can be obtained through the ABPP Web site).

The academies of each specialty function independently from the specialty boards, although close, collegial communication and cooperation between the specialty board and its academy likely supports the greater good of the specialty (and psychology in general). The academy is the membership body of that specialty. Each academy has a board of officers (generally, a president, vice-president/president-elect, treasurer, and secretary) that serve as volunteers to support the activities of that academy. Some well-established academies, such as Forensic Psychology and Clinical Neuropsychology, offer well-received continuing education programs along with other activities such as advocacy for the specialty. Academies are also charged with providing leadership in recruitment of potential candidates for ABPP certification. By maintaining your membership in your specialty's academy you can become actively involved in the ongoing activities provided by the academies, such as continuing education, mentoring, advocacy activities, recruitment, and improving quality and accessibility of services in the specialty.

In most academies, board membership is determined by consistent involvement and interest in board-related activities. If the academy does not have a listserv through which you can learn about opportunities for involvement, you can contact members of the academy board to express your interest and offer to assist in academy activities. To become active in either academy or specialty-board leadership, it is important to express your interest, make yourself reasonably available when assistance is requested, and demonstrate reliability in carrying out any assigned tasks.

Summary

It is up to you to decide what to do after you receive your ABPP board certification. The psychology profession and the ABPP need you to advance the future of the profession by being an advocate for ABPP board certification and assisting the organization through activities such as mentorship and serving as an examiner. The ABPP defines professionals who have met advanced qualifications and standards of competence in the specialties of psychology. You can help spread the word about the ABPP and what it represents, and can encourage others to strive for similar levels of excellence. In the end, promotion of the ABPP as a standard that every psychologist should reach will help maintain the status of the psychology profession.

To stay in touch with the ABPP and your academy, visit the ABPP Web site. Through that site, you can find contact information for the officers of each specialty board and for most of the academies (academy presidents and their contact information is listed along with specialty-board members). Currently, this information is listed under the Governance/Central Office tab, at the Specialty Board link. You might also consider searching the academy name through a search engine; many of the academies have detailed Web sites that contain information about the organization, as well as information about and links to other specialty resources.

Professional Development and Lifelong Learning

A. J Finch, Jr., PhD, ABPP
Specialties in Clinical and Clinical
Child & Adolescent Psychology

Introduction

This chapter is about professional development and lifelong learning. For purposes of simplicity, the term *professional development* is used throughout and is defined as a "developmental process of acquiring, expanding, refining, and sustaining knowledge, proficiency, skill, and qualifications for competent professional function" (Elman, Illfelder-Kaye, & Robiner, 2005, p. 368). A couple of important issues are raised by this definition.

First, professional development is an ongoing process, not a goal. As professionals we are continuously developing and never fully completing the process.

Second, the issue of learning new information, expanding our knowledge base, and sustaining the knowledge we have is particularly important in the rapidly changing field of professional psychology. A quick look at the number of journals and publications in the field clearly demonstrates the size of the information explosion. If one spends some time wandering through the American Psychological Association (APA) bookstore or publisher exhibits during an APA convention, the large number of topics and new information can be a bit overwhelming. Such an experience tends to remind us that there is much information from graduate school that we leave behind if we do not use it in our everyday professional life.

Another issue raised by the definition of professional development relates to sustaining professional skills and proficiencies. When was the last time someone actually observed your interactions with a client? Much of what we do as professional psychologists goes on behind closed doors. How do we know when our skills have begun to erode and we have become sloppy in the use of test instruments or interviewing techniques?

Finally, the issue of qualifications is a particularly important one for those who have obtained, or are considering obtaining, board certification through the ABPP. How do we know a psychologist is qualified in a particular area? Few of us would consider having surgery without first checking the qualifications of our surgeon. Is this person a specialist in the area? Hospitals generally require the physician to be board certified to have hospital privileges. By contrast, relatively few psychologists seek to become board-certified specialists through the ABPP. Certainly ABPP board certification is the clearest and most respected demonstration of qualification to practice in a specialty area. Without a sufficient number of ABPP-certified clinicans available, however, there exists a significant gap in the that people may recognize competent psychology specialists.

Professional Development

As a board-certified specialist your educational needs and goals become less clear than they were earlier in your career. Some minimum direction may be provided by your state regulations. According to Sharkin and Plageman (2003), 41 states and the District of Columbia require continuing education (CE) for licensure renewal. As a result, most board-certified psychologists will need to seek CE credits to maintain their practice. However, in most states little direction is provided by these requirements. It is this lack of direction and lack of demonstrated effectiveness of CE that has led some to question the purpose of mandatory CE. Even with these concerns, Sharkin and Plageman (2003) found in their survey of licensed psychologists that most psychologists supported CE requirements and generally found them useful. Moreover, a carefully prepared professional development plan makes CE even more meaningful and useful.

Regardless of whether CE requirements exist for licensure in your state, as a board-certified psychologist you should define your educational or professional development goals. Elman and colleagues (2005) have suggested that professional development for the experienced psychologist should be conceptualized as an ongoing developmental process through retirement. They emphasize the importance of the personal development of the psychologist and see this focus as the foundation of a prevention model of professional practice. The personal development of the psychologist encourages reflection, ongoing learning, critical thinking, and self-care.

One way of working on personal development is through a peer supervision or consultation group. Peer supervision groups provide a safe environment in which the members can explore and develop as individuals and as psychologists. In order to provide this safe environment, peer group supervision participants have to establish trust among the members, rules of confidentiality, a sense of mutual appreciation, and an atmosphere of mutual respect. These groups provide a sounding board for exploring various issues and gaining feedback from others in a safe and nonjudgmental environment. Issues of transference and countertransference are frequently dealt with in these groups. Blind spots can be identified and dealt with in this safe environment. Interpersonal and individual problems as well as weaknesses and difficulties are also discussed. In addition, other members of the group can provide the psychologist with different perspectives to approaching problems and dealing with practice issues such as between-session calls and billing.

Other advantages of peer supervision groups are that they can decrease professional isolation, increase social support, decrease the stress of practice, and help in the development of networking. One potential issue that may present a problem to some individuals is that most such supervision groups do not provide formal CE credit. Some individuals have been able to receive formal CE credit for such groups; these groups are usually associated with a university or medical school.

In addition to this focus on the personal development of the psychologist, I would suggest a continued need for the acquiring of new knowledge and skills. Psychology is a dynamic field, and the changes that are rapidly coming make it critical that psychologists learn new information and skills. Some peer supervision groups contain a didactic component, but most teaching takes place in other formats such as CE workshops and readings.

Developing Competencies

How do you determine what areas of new knowledge and skills you should develop? Keep in mind that the major reason for the development of new skills and the acquiring of new knowledge is to increase competencies. There has been increasing discussion on competencies and the assessment of competencies in a variety of fields including professional psychology (Kaslow, 2004; Kaslow et al., 2006) A brief overview of the competencies in professional psychology will help focus your professional development plan.

Competencies are made up of knowledge, skills, and attitudes needed for professional practice (Kaslow, 2004). Although an extensive discussion of competencies in presented in Chapter 3, several points regarding competences are repeated here. Each of the specialty boards of the ABPP examines for these competencies, and the organization has been one of the leaders in the area of the assessment of competencies. Psychological competencies are divided into foundational competencies and core competencies. Foundational competencies include ethics, and individual and cultural diversity. The foundational competencies are underlying beliefs and principles that guide professional behavior. They are more than simply being familiar with the ethical code or knowing about various ethnic or minority groups. They constitute an acute sensitivity and constant awareness of the unique issues involved with each individual one serves.

Similarly, one of the core competencies has to do with "scientific mindfulness." Our behaviors are guided by scientific knowledge, and we see ourselves as scientific problem solvers. We approach problems with an empirical and rational attitude. We are constantly generating and testing hypotheses and evaluating them on the basis of theory we have developed about each individual patient. This scientific underpinning guides the other core competencies in psychological assessment, intervention, consultation, supervision, and professional development. In Chapter 3, Kaslow and Ingram provide a detailed discussion of these areas. This chapter revisits these competencies because they can provide a guiding framework as you begin to develop a plan for your professional development.

In planning professional development it is important to determine whether you should focus mainly on your particular specialty area or on generic applied psychological knowledge. It could be argued that the rapid rate at which new findings are appearing in some specialty areas makes it very difficult to keep up in that one area, thus you should focus on the specialty area. Others would suggest that it is more helpful to keep up with the broader field of psychology. Regardless, both foci are important, as each specialty area is dependent on broader knowledge. No matter what your specialty area, it is important to keep an eye on the field as a whole.

It is not suggested here that you focus equally on all areas. However, you cannot ignore other areas outside of your specialty area. For example, a clinical neuropsychologist cannot ignore what is going on in the general clinical field any more than a clinical psychologist can ignore the neuropsychology area. A specialist in group psychology cannot be ill-informed about marital and couple issues. Clients do not present for treatment presorted. Basic knowledge across the field of professional psychology is necessary to provide competent services. You have to set goals in both your specialty area and in the broader field of professional psychology to direct your professional development.

Chapter 5 makes an interesting point about never knowing what direction your practice may ultimately lead you. Given this truth, strategic planning is necessary. Without some plan for your professional development, you are likely to find yourself randomly acquiring CE credits and reading the literature without making the most of the opportunities available to you. Considering this, it becomes clear that developing a plan is a good idea.

SWOT Analysis as an Aid to Developing Your Plan

It may be helpful to borrow from the world of business and develop a SWOT analysis to aid in your professional development plan. A SWOT analysis involves the development of a list of potential strengths (S), weaknesses (W), opportunities (O), and threats (T). The process might go something like this. First, come up with a realistic list of your particular strengths as a psychological specialist. You obviously have skills in the area in which you are board certified. However, you are likely to have some particular areas of really well-developed skills. What are they? Here a review of the foundational and core competencies can serve as a guide. In which of these areas are you most fully developed and up to date? What do you need to do to keep this edge?

Now that you have a list of your strengths, develop a realistic list of your weaknesses. In which of these competencies areas do you need to improve? In what area do you feel most insecure? I have a friend who felt really inadequate in his knowledge of statistics and that his lack of knowledge limited his ability to understand some of the scientific foundations. He set out to learn more about statistics on his own. He consulted with colleagues, attended workshops, and read extensively. Eventually he became the person most people in the department turned to with their questions on statistics. Similarly, a child psychologist felt inadequately prepared to work with marital issues. She felt that knowledge and skill in this area were important for her interventions with children and their families. Her caseload seemed to be full of such issues. She sought supervision, attended workshops in the area, and began to read extensively on the topic. Now she frequently is the first person that many psychologists in her region think of when referring clients with marital issues. Both of these individuals turned a perceived weakness into a strength by developing a professional development plan and following through with it. However, first they had to identify their perceived weaknesses.

What are the opportunities available for you? Is there a particular need in your community that you realistically could meet with some additional training or knowledge? Are there programs in your community that you might be able to attend to expand your competencies? A friend of mine had a practice that was heavily assessment oriented. He recognized the need to know more about learning disabilities and enrolled in the school psychology program in the area. Eventually he earned his Ed.S. For various reasons he decided to leave full-time private practice and took a job with the local school system as a school psychologist. He took advantage of an opportunity in the community to address a weakness in one of his competence areas and it facilitated a career move for him.

Finally, what are the potential threats to your practice in professional psychology? Certainly for many psychologists there are many such threats, ranging from managed care to increased competition from other professions. How can you address these potential threats through a professional development plan? With the limited number of sessions covered by many managed-care plans, it might be beneficial to focus on more empirically supported treatment programs that tend to be more problem focused and time limited. Another possibility might be to focus on areas that are not dependent on managed care. For example, one psychologist I know began to focus on gifted children by attending workshops, reading, and seeking consultation in the area. Eventually he was able to expand his practice into the assessment of children for admission to classes for the gifted. Although this clientele did not make up his total caseload, it did help to soften the blow of decreased payment from managed care, because these services were not covered by insurance and were totally self-pay.

Another psychologist gradually moved his totally therapy-based practice to one that focused heavily on custody evaluations. He did not simply make this change in his practice; rather, he planned it by seeking workshops, reading, and supervision in the area. In addition to the ethical issues involved, he would not have been able to survive in this emotionally charged and legally contentious area without adequate preparation. However, he planned and prepared for the change and has been practicing successfully for years in the field.

Summary

The development of a SWOT plan for professional development helps structure the process and makes it more meaningful. Without planning, too many psychologists are likely to find themselves nearing the deadline for mandatory CE units and taking whatever offerings are available. A word of caution is needed here. Considerable awareness and information can be acquired through the workshops; however, simply attending workshops does not necessarily prepare a psychologist to practice in a particular area. Supervision and consultation are also needed in the development of a new or expanded competency area.

Pitfalls to Avoid

Arthur M. Nezu, PhD, ABPP
Specialties in Clinical and Cognitive
& Behavioral Psychology

Introduction

We are always being told (or else telling our clients or patients) to "see the forest from the trees!"—in other words, to be certain to remember the "big picture" or meta-message when we attempt to understand a problem, tackle a new challenge, or undertake a new task. Such advice cautions us to keep the "big picture in mind" constantly while we are dealing with the smaller pieces of the picture. Otherwise, we may lose sight of the overall message or goal.

However, rather than vociferously advocating that you need to focus on the big picture, this chapter underscores the importance of paying close attention to detail while going through the process of applying and obtaining ABPP certification. Within this context, this chapter is different from the others in the book, in that it provides a laundry list of "do's and don'ts" with regard to the application process itself, preparation of a practice sample, preparation for the oral exam, and taking of the oral exam.

The lists were generated by asking various members of the ABPP leadership and ABPP examiners to identify frequent mistakes, oversights, and outright errors they encountered in their evaluative roles during the various stages of the application and examination process. Although some of the suggestions appear rather obvious or even silly, they are included because of their frequency as noted by various ABPP administrators, credential reviewers, practice sample coordinators, oral exam chairs, and others involved in the review process. As such, this chapter is presented in the spirit of helping applicants and candidates to avoid such pitfalls so that the goal of becoming board certified is realized with a minimal amount of frustration, angst, and hassles.

Preparing the Initial Application

1. Be neat—if you are not using a word-processing program to complete any of the application materials, make sure that your handwriting is legible (this sounds silly, but too often, mistakes in return addresses are due to poor penmanship).
2. Proofread all application materials for spelling and grammatical errors—use the "spell-check" function if relevant.
3. Answer *all* questions on the application forms. Provide necessary contact information (e.g., office, home, and mobile phone numbers; current e-mail addresses). When submitting a CV as part of the application, be sure to update it, revise it if necessary to highlight relevant information pertinent to the ABPP, and be specific.
4. Provide the types of information and documentation that demonstrate that you meet all stated requirements for a given specialty board.
5. Provide *accurate* information about your credentials (e.g., correct dates, correct names of training sites and relevant supervisors). One credentials reviewer noted that a recent applicant submitted the following information concerning a completed APA-accredited internship: "Internship, ABC Hospital, APA accredited Sept 1 1995 to Aug 1993." What does this actually mean? Such a minor mistake can lead to significant time delays.
6. Be truthful. Very few applicants attempt to deliberately provide false information, but be careful to not "fudge" information (e.g., the year that your program was accredited; the name of the program that you graduated from).

Preparing the Practice Sample and Accompanying Written Documents

1. Pay attention to the specified due dates for materials.
2. Send in the fee for this step to the ABPP central office in a timely manner.
3. Ask questions of a mentor if your specialty board offers this service.

4. Choose a practice sample that represents a good example of what you typically do in your everyday professional work. You do not have to pick a highly interesting, successful, exotic, or unusual case. For example, if you currently and regularly treat adults who present with anxiety disorders, it is probably not a good idea to use the one case of an adolescent whom you diagnosed with borderline personality disorder during your internship several years ago.

5. Eliminate any patient-identifying information on any of the practice sample materials. A crucial ethical concern for all psychologists is to guard against threats to a patient's confidentiality. Make sure you convey adherence to this principle in everything you do.

6. Review all practice sample materials for completeness (e.g., correct number of copies requested, answering all questions), spelling errors, neatness, and relevance before you send them off to the relevant practice sample coordinator.

7. Proofread all practice sample materials for spelling and grammatical errors.

8. Provide relevant contact information on all materials.

9. Provide audiotapes or videotapes that are part of the practice sample that are of *high sound and picture quality*.

10. Include only relevant materials. For example, if your practice sample involves a consultation case, provide only the material that is relevant to the client in question, not reams of paper about the organization.

11. Remember who your client is—in working with an organization, for example, the client may be the organization, but you might actually be working with various employees. Be careful to describe how you maintained correct boundaries.

12. Use tests and assessment instruments in the manner in which they were originally designed and validated. For example, do not use part of a test to help make a diagnosis or treatment decision unless there is sound justification.

Continued

Preparing the Practice Sample and Accompanying Written Documents *(Continued)*

13. Be patient. Unless your specialty board offers prescheduled exam dates, remember that it might be some time before your examination chair is able to put together an appropriate exam committee for you, especially of you live in an area of the country where few board-certified psychologists reside.

Preparing for the Oral Exam

1. Pay attention to the specified due dates for materials.
2. Send in the fee for this step to the ABPP central office in a timely manner.
3. Intimately review your practice sample before the oral examination. Exam committee members are not impressed if you forget crucial details about the case you included as part of your sample.
4. Remember that much of what will be discussed at the examination will be *what* it is you do and *how* you go about doing it.
5. Remember that this is generally a standardized exam. Everyone else is being asked to do the same job.
6. Review the APA ethics code!
7. If you know members of your exam committee ahead of time, you may wish to become familiar with whom they are. But don't spend too much time doing so; they will be more interested in you and your work and will not evaluate you according to how much you know about them.
8. Be sure to become familiar with diversity issues related to your specialty.

Taking the Oral Exam

1. Arrive early for the exam. Take into account busy travel times (e.g., traffic jams). Consider staying at a hotel or motel the night before to cut down on travel time (this helps to reduce anxiety as well!).
2. Answer the question that is being asked. This is not an interview for political office in which one tries to reframe the inquiry to answer a question of choice. Nor should you try to "read" something into the question that is not intended. There will be no "trick questions!"
3. Respond to questions that you don't know how to answer with "I'm not familiar with that concept [author, research study]" if this is true. Do not try to bluff or make excuses—you are not expected to know everything!
4. Be confident, not arrogant or overbearing.
5. Remember that this is a professional setting. It is highly likely that your exam committee will perceive your interpersonal interactions with them as potentially representing your interpersonal interactions with both clients or patients and other professionals.
6. Do not equate a patient or client with his or her diagnosis (e.g., "so, my depressive begins to cry when he was asked about his recent firing").
7. Remember that you are being evaluated for meeting a minimal level of competency in a particular specialty. You do not need to overwhelm or dazzle your exam committee and make them believe you are the best!
8. Be ready to acknowledge problems with your case and any related weaknesses or limitations; volunteer what you may have learned from this case and how you might do something different in hindsight.

After the Oral Examination

1. Congrats—the oral exam is over! Now, as in all things worth waiting for, remember to be patient for the results. Different boards have various ways of communicating the results of the exam. Your board may need a few days to get in touch with you.

2. Please do not formally use any title associated with the ABPP until you are officially notified of passing the exam. There is no official status of being an ABPP candidate. Use of any title prematurely may be an ethics violation.

3. Remember to continue to pay your annual attestation fees once you have become board certified!

4. Consider becoming a member of your specialty's academy.

5. Consider becoming more involved in your specialty's board (e.g., member of the Board of Directors, examiner).

References

American Board of Examiners in Professional Psychology. (1947a). *ABEPP minutes of September* 9–13, 1947. Detroit, MI: Author.

American Board of Examiners in Professional Psychology. (1947b). *ABEPP minutes of December* 19–21, 1947. Columbus, OH: Author.

American Board of Examiners in Professional Psychology. (1949). *ABEPP minutes of March* 5–7, 1949. Chicago, IL: Author.

American Board of Professional Psychology. (1972). *January Minutes of the Mid-Winter Meeting of the Board of Trustees.* Columbia, MO: Authors.

American Board of Professional Psychology. (1992). ABPP at 45 [Special Section]. *Diplomate,* 12(1), 5–13.

American Board of Professional Psychology. (1997a). ABPP at 50 [Special Section]. *Diplomate,* 17(1), 11–24.

American Board of Professional Psychology. (1997b). *Application manual for specialty board affiliation.* Columbia, MO: Author.

American Board of Professional Psychology. (1997c). *Standards manual for specialty boards, candidacy, and examinations.* Columbia, MO: Author.

American Board of Professional Psychology (1998–2007). *Minutes of the Annual Meeting of the Board of Trustees.* Columbia, MO and Savannah, GA: Author.

American Board of Professional Psychology (2007, Winter). The contributions of Manfred Meier: Special section. *The Specialist,* 26, 8–10.

American Board of Professional Psychology (2008). *ABPP Value statement.* Retrieved June 25, 2008, from http://www.abpp.org.

American Board of Professional Psychology (2009). *ABPP Policies and Procedures,* Retrieved February 10, 2009, from http://www.abpp.org.

American Psychiatric Association. (2000). *Diagnostic and Statistical Manual of Mental Disorders,* 4th ed., text revision. (DSM-IV-TR). Washington, DC: Author.

American Psychological Association. (1946). *Report of the Policy and Planning Board on Certification of Professional Psychologists* (Vol. 1, p. 41). Washington, DC: Author.

American Psychological Association. (2002). Ethical principles of psychologists and code of conduct. *American Psychologist,* 57, 1060–1073.

American Psychological Association. (2003). Guidelines on multicultural education, training, research, practice, and organizational change for psychologists. *American Psychologist,* 58, 377–402.

American Psychological Association. (2004). Guidelines for psychological practice with older adults. *American Psychologist,* 59, 236–260.

American Psychological Association. (2007). *Guidelines for psychological practice with girls and women: A Joint Task Force of APA Divisions 17 and 35.* Washington, DC: Author.

Antony, M. M., Orsillo, S. M., & Roemer, L. (2001). *Practitioner's guide to empirically based measures of anxiety.* New York: Kluwer Academic Plenum Publishers.

Armstrong, K. E., Beebe, D. W., Hilsabeck, R. C. & Kirkwood, M. W. (2008). *Board certification in clinical neuropsychology: A guide to becoming ABPP/ABCN certified without sacrificing your sanity.* New York: Oxford University Press.

Arredondo, P., Shealy, C., Neale, M. C., & Winfrey, L. L. (2004). Consultation and interprofessional collaboration: Modeling for the future. *Journal of Clinical Psychology,* 80, 787–800.

Arredondo, P., Toporek, R., Brown, S. B., Jones, J., Locke, D. C., Sanchez, J., & Stadler, H. (1996). Operationalization of the multicultural counseling competencies. *Journal of Multicultural Counseling and Development,* 24, 42–78.

Association of State and Provincial Psychology Boards (2008). *Instructions to apply for a certificate of professional qualification in psychology (CPQ) or to deposit information in the ASPPB credentials bank.* Retrieved July 29, 2008, from http://www.asppb.org/mobility/pdf/forms/Instructions.pdf

Bandiera, G., Sherbino, J., & Frank, J. R. (Eds.). (2006). *The CanMEDS assessment tools handbook: An introductory guide to assessment methods for the CanMEDS competencies.* Ottawa, Ontario: The Royal College of Physicians and Surgeons of Canada.

Belar, C. D., Brown, R. A., Hersch, L. E., Hornyak, L. M., Rozensky, R. H., Sheridan, E. P., Brown, R. T., & Reed, G. W. (2001). Self-assessment in clinical health psychology: A model for ethical expansion of practice. *Professional Psychology: Research and Practice,* 32, 135–141.

Bent, R. J. (1986). Toward quality control in the education of practicing psychologists. In J. A. Callan, D. R. Peterson, & G. A. Stricker (Eds.), *Quality in professional training* (pp. 82–98). Norman, OK: Transcript Press.

Bent, R. J. (1992). The professional core competency areas. In R. L. Peterson, J. D. McHolland, R. J. Bent, E. Russell-Davis, & G. E. Edwall (Eds.), *The core curriculum in professional psychology* (pp. 77–81). Washington, DC: American Psychological Association.

Bent, R. J., & Cannon, W. G. (1987). Key functional skills of professional psychologists. In E. F. Bourg, R. J. Bent, J. E. Callan, N. F. Jones, J. McHolland, & G. Stricker (Eds.), *Standards and evaluation in the education and training of professional psychologists: Knowledge, attitudes, and skills* (pp. 87–98). Norman, OK: Transcript Press.

Bent, R. J., Packard, R. E., & Goldberg, R. W. (1999). The American Board of Professional Psychology, 1947 to 1997: A historical perspective. *Professional Psychology: Research and Practice, 30,* 65–73.

Berg, C. A., & Upchurch, R. (2007). A developmental-contextual model of couples coping with chronic illness across the adult lifespan. *Psychological Bulletin, 133,* 920–954.

Bieschke, K. J., Fouad, N. A., Collins, F. L., & Halonen, J. S. (2004). The scientifically minded psychologist: Science as a core competency. *Journal of Clinical Psychology,* 80, 713–724.

Blumenfeld, H. (2002). *Neuroanatomy through clinical cases.* Sunderland, MA: Sinauer Associates.

Bourg, E. F., Bent, R. J., Callan, J. E., Jones, N. F., McHolland, J. D., & Stricker, G. (Eds.). (1987). *Standards and evaluation in the education and training of professional psychologists.* Norman, OK: Transcript Press.

Bourg, E. F., Bent, R. J., McHolland, J. D., & Stricker, G. (1989). Standards and evaluation in the accreditation and training of professional psychologists: The National Council of Schools of Professional Psychology. *American Psychologist, 44,* 66–72.

Carver, C. S. (2002). Resilience and thriving: Issues, models, and linkages. *Journal of Social Issues,* 54, 245–266.

Chapman, R. A. (2005). Stage of change model as applied to the diplomate process. *The Specialist, Winter Edition, Vol.* 24, 1, 11ff.

Cubic, B. A., & Gatewood, E. E. (2008). ACGME core competencies: Helpful information for psychologists. *Journal of Clinical Psychology in Medical Settings,* 15, 28–39.

Connell, M., Conroy, M. A., & Witt, P. (2006). Key legal cases in forensic mental health. Sarasota, FL: Professional Resource Press.

Dattilio, F. M. (2002). Board Certification in Psychology: Is it really necessary? *Professional Psychology: Research and Practice,* 33, 1, 54–57.

de las Fuentes, C., Willmuth, M. E., & Yarrow, C. (2005). Ethics education: The development of competence, past and present. *Professional Psychology: Research and Practice,* 36, 362–366.

Division 44. (2000). Guidelines for psychotherapy with lesbian, gay, and bisexual clients. *American Psychologist,* 55, 1440–1451.

Doverspike, W. F. (1999). *Ethical risk management.* Sarasota, FL: Professional Resource Press.

Elman, N. S., Illfelder-Kaye, K., & Robiner, W.N. (2005). Professional development: Training for professionalism as a foundation for competent practice in psychology. *Professional Psychology: Research and Practice*, 36, 367–375.

Epstein, R. M. (2007). Assessment in medical education. *New England Journal of Medicine,* 356, 387–396.

Epstein, R. M., & Hundert, E. M. (2002). Defining and assessing professional competence. *Journal of the American Medical Association,* 287, 226–235.

Falender, C. A., Cornish, J. A. E., Goodyear, R., Hatcher, R., Kaslow, N. J., Leventhal, G., Shafranske, E., Sigmon, S. T., Stoltenberg, C., & Grus, C. (2004). Defining competencies in psychology supervision: A consensus statement. *Journal of Clinical Psychology,* 80, 771–786.

Falender, C. A., & Shafranske, E. (2004). *Clinical supervision: A competency-based approach.* Washington, DC. American Psychological Association.

Falender, C. A., & Shafranske, E. P. (2007). Competence in competency-based supervision practice: Construct and application. *Professional Psychology: Research and Practice,* 38, 232–240.

Finch, A. J., Simon, M. P., & Nezu, C. M. (2006). The future of clinical psychology: Board certification. *Clinical Psychology: Science and Practice,* 13, 254–257.

Folkman, S., Lazarus, S. M., Dunkel-Shelter, C., DeLongis, A., & Gruen, R. J. (1986). Dynamics of a stressful encounter: Cognitive appraisal, coping, and encounter outcomes. *Journal of Personality and Social Psychology,* 50, 992–1003.

Fraser, S. W., & Greenhalgh, T. (2001). Coping with complexity: Educating for capability. *British Medical Journal,* 323, 799–803.

Goldstein, A. (Ed.) (2002). *Forensic psychology.* New York: Wiley.

Grisso, T. (Ed.) (2003). *Evaluating competencies: Forensic assessments and instruments* (2nd ed.). New York: Kluwer/Plenum.

Hannay, H. J., Bieliauskas, L. A., Crosson, B. A., Hammeke, T. A., Hamsher, K. deS., & Koffler, S. (Eds.) (1998). Proceedings of the Houston Conference on Specialty Education and Training in Clinical Neuropsychology: Policy statement. *Archives of Clinical Neuropsychology,* 13, 160–166.

Hatcher, R. L., & Lassiter, K. D. (2007). Initial training in professional psychology: The practicum competencies outline. *Training and Education in Professional Psychology,* 1, 49–63.

Heilbrun, K. (2001). *Principles of forensic mental health assessment.* New York: Kluwer/ Plenum.

Heilman, K.M. & Valenstein, E. (Eds.). (2003). *Clinical neuropsychology* (4th ed.). New York: Oxford University Press.

Hoge, M. A., Morris, J. A., Daniels, A. S., Huey, L. Y., Stuart, G. W., Adams, N., Paris, M., Goplerud, E., Horgan, C. M., Kaplan, L., Storti, S. A., & Dodge, J. M. (2005). Report of recommendations: The Annapolis Coalition on Behavioral Health Work Force Competencies. *Administration and Policy in Mental Health,* 32, 651–663.

Honk, J. V., & Schutter, D. J. (2006). Unmasked feigned sanity: A neurobiological model of emotional processing in primary psychopathy. *Cognitive Neuropsychiatry,* 11, 285–306.

Kaslow, N. J. (2004). Competencies in professional psychology. *American Psychologist,* 59, 774–781.

Kaslow, N. J., & Bell, K. D. (2008). A competency-based approach to supervision. In C. A. Falendar & E. P. Shafranske (Eds.), *Casebook for clinical supervision: A competency-based approach* (pp. 17–38). Washington, DC: American Psychological Association.

Kaslow, N. J., Borden, K. A., Collins, F. L., Forrest, L., Illfelder-Kaye, J., Nelson, P. D., Rallo, J. S., Vasquez, M. J. T., & Willmuth, M. E. (2004). Competencies Conference: Future directions in education and credentialing in professional psychology. *Journal of Clinical Psychology,* 80, 699–712.

Kaslow, N. J., Dunn, S. E., & Smith, C. O. (2008). Competencies for psychologists in academic health centers (AHCs). *Journal of Clinical Psychology in Medical Settings,* 15, 18–27.

Kaslow, N. J., Rubin, N. J., Bebeau, M., Leigh, I. W., Lichtenberg, J., Nelson, P. D., Portnoy, S., & Smith, I. L. (2007). Guiding principles and recommendations for the assessment of competence. *Professional Psychology: Research and Practice,* 38, 441–451.

Kaslow, N. J., Rubin, N. J., Leigh, I. W., Portnoy, S., Lichenberg, J., Smith, I. L., Bebeau, M., & Nelson, P. D. (2006). *American Psychological Association Task Force on the Assessment of Competence in Professional Psychology.* Washington, DC: American Psychological Association.

Kitchener, K. S. (2000). *Foundations of ethical practice, research, and teaching in psychology.* Mahwah, NJ: Erlbaum.

Kolb, B., & Whishaw, I. Q. (2003). *Fundamentals of human neuropsychology* (5th ed.). New York: Worth Publishers.

Krishnamurthy, R., Vandecreek, L., Kaslow, N. J., Tazeau, Y. N., Milville, M. L., Kerns, R., Stegman, R., Suzuki, L. A., & Benton, S. A. (2004). Achieving competency in psychological assessment: Directions for education and training. *Journal of Clinical Psychology,* 80, 725–740.

Leigh, I. W., Smith, I. L., Bebeau, M., Lichtenberg, J., Nelson, P. D., Portnoy, S., Rubin, N. J., & Kaslow, N. J. (2007). Competency assessment models. *Professional Psychology: Research and Practice,* 38, 463–473.

Lichtenberg, J., Portnoy, S., Bebeau, M., Leigh, I. W., Nelson, P. D., Rubin, N. J., Smith, I. L., & Kaslow, N. J. (2007). Challenges to the assessment of competence and competencies. *Professional Psychology: Research and Practice, 38*, 474–478.

Locke, D. C. (1992). *Increasing multicultural understanding: A comprehensive model. Multicultural aspects of counseling Series 1.* Newbury Park, CA: Sage Publications.

Manthei, R. J. (1996). A follow-up study of clients who fail to begin counseling or terminate after one session. *International Journal for the Advancement of Counseling, 18*, 115–128.

May, R. J. (1991). Effects of waiting for clinical service on attrition, problem resolution, satisfaction, attitudes toward psychotherapy and treatment outcome: A review of the literature. *Professional Psychology: Research and Practice, 22*, 209–214.

Mayfield, P. N. (1987). Certification of psychologists by the American Board of Professional Psychology. In B. A. Edelstein & E. S. Berler (Eds.), *Evaluation and accountability in clinical training* (pp. 283–297). New York: Plenum Press.

Melton, G. B., Petrila, J., Poythress, N. G., Slobogin, C., Lyons, P., & Otto, R. K. (2007). *Psychological evaluations for the courts: A handbook for mental health professionals and lawyers* (3rd ed). New York: Guilford.

Morgan, J. E. & Ricker, J. H. (Eds.). (2008). *Textbook of clinical neuropsychology.* New York: Oxford University Press.

Nelson, W. M., III, & Finch, A. J., Jr. (2005). Board certification and professional psychology: A developmental passage. *San Francisco Psychologist*, December, 11 ff.

Nezu, A. M., Nezu, C. M., Friedman, S. H., & Haynes, S. N. (1998). Case formulation in behavior therapy: problem solving and functional analytic strategies. In T. D. Eells (Ed.), *Handbook of psychotherapy case formulation* (pp. 368–401). New York: Guilford.

Nezu, A. M., Ronan, G. F., Meadows, E. A., & McClure, K. S. (Eds.) (2000). *Practitioner's guide to empirically based measures of depression.* New York: Kluwer Academic/Plenum.

Oxford English Dictionary. (2006). *Competence.* Oxford, UK: Oxford University Press.

Packard, T., & Reyes, C. J. (2003). Specialty certification in professional psychology. In M. J. Prinstein & M. D. Patterson (Eds.), *The portable mentor: Expert guide to a successful career in psychology* (pp. 191–208). New York: Plenum.

Peterson, R. L., McHolland, J. D., Bent, R. J., David-Russell, E., Edwall, G. E., Polite, K., Singer, D. R., & Stricker, G. (1992). *The core curriculum in professional psychology.* Washington, DC: American Psychological Association.

Prochaska, J. O., DiClemente, C. C., & Norcross, J. (1998). Stages of change: Prescriptive guidelines for behavior medicine and psychotherapy. In G. P. Koocher, J. C. Norcross, & S. S. Hill, (Eds.), *Psychologists' Desk Reference* (pp. 230–235). New York: Oxford University Press.

Prochaska, J. O., & Velicer, N. F. (1997). Behavior change: The transtheoretical model of health behavior change. *American Journal of Health Promotion, 12*, 38–48.

Reitzel, L. R., Stellrecht, N. E., Gordon, K. H., Lima, E. N., Wingate, L. R., Brown, J. S., et al. (2006). Does time between application and case assignment predict therapy attendance or premature termination in outpatients? *Psychological Services, 3*, 51–60.

Roberts, M. C., Borden, K. A., Christiansen, M. D., & Lopez, S. J. (2005). Fostering a culture shift: Assessment of competence in the education and careers of professional psychologists. *Professional Psychology: Research and Practice, 36*, 355–361.

Rodolfa, E. R., Bent, R. J., Eisman, E., Nelson, P. D., Rehm, L., & Ritchie, P. (2005). A cube model for competency development: Implications for psychology educators and regulators. *Professional Psychology: Research and Practice, 36*, 347–354.

Rubin, N. J., Bebeau, M., Leigh, I. W., Lichtenberg, J., Smith, I. L., Nelson, P. D., Portnoy, S., & Kaslow, N. J. (2007). The competency movement within psychology: An historical perspective. *Professional Psychology: Research and Practice, 38*, 452–462.

Sales, B., Bricklin, P., & Hall, J. (1984). *Specialization in psychology: Principles (November 1984 Draft)*. Washington, DC: American Psychological Association.

Sellers, R. M., Smith, M. A., Shelton, J. N., Rowley, S. A., Sellers, and Chavous, T. M. (1998). Multidimensional model of racial identity: A reconceptualization of African-American racial identity. *Personality and Social Psychology Review, 2*, 18–39.

Sharkin, B. S., & Plageman, P. M. (2003). What do psychologists think about mandatory continuing education? A survey of Pennsylvania practitioners. *Professional Psychology: Research and Practice, 34*, 318–323.

Spruill, J., Rozensky, R. H., Stigall, T. T., Vasquez, M., Binghman, R. P., & Olvey, C. D. (2004). Becoming a competent clinician: Basic competencies in intervention. *Journal of Clinical Psychology, 80*, 741–754.

Stephenson, J., & Yorke, M. (Eds.). (1998). *Capability and quality in higher education*. London: Kogan Page.

Stern, D. T. (Ed.). (2006). *Measuring medical professionalism*. Oxford: Oxford University Press.

Sweet, J. J., Nelson, N. W., & Moberg, P. J. (2006). The TCN/AACN 2005 "salary survey": professional practices, beliefs, and incomes of U.S. neuropsychologists. *Clinical Neuropsychologist, 20*, 325–364.

Valentiner, D. P., Holahan, C. J., & Moos, R. H. (1994). Social support, appraisals of event controllability, and coping: An integrative model. *Journal of Personality and Social Psychology, 66*, 1094–1102.

Willis, S. L., & Dubin, S. S. (Eds.). (1990). *Maintaining professional competence: Approaches to career enhancement, vitality, and success throughout a work life*. San Francisco: Jossey-Bass.

Willner, P., Muscat, R., & Papp, M. (1992). Chronic mild stress-induced anhedonia: a realistic animal model of depression. *Neuroscience and Biobehavioral Reviews, 16*, 525–534.